THE BOOK

OF THE

SECRETS OF ENOCH

TRANSLATED FROM THE SLAVONIC

BY

W. R. MORFILL, M.A.

READER IN RUSSIAN AND THE OTHER SLAVONIC LANGUAGES

AND

EDITED, WITH INTRODUCTION, NOTES AND INDICES

BY

R. H. CHARLES, M.A.

TRINITY COLLEGE, DUBLIN, AND EXETER COLLEGE, OXFORD

Oxford

AT THE CLARENDON PRESS

1896

ISBN 978-1-58509-505-6

𝕺𝔵𝔣𝔬𝔯𝔡

Published by

**The Book Tree
Post Office Box 724
Escondido, CA 92033**

Call (800) 700-TREE for a FREE BOOK TREE CATALOG
with over 1000 Books, Booklets, Audio, and Video on
Alchemy, Ancient Mysteries, Anti-Gravity, Atlantis, Free
Energy, Gnosticism, Health Issues, Magic, Metaphysics,
Mythology, Occult, Rare Books, Religious Controversy,
Sitchin Studies, Spirituality, Symbolism, Tesla, and much
more. Or visit our website at www.thebooktree.com

HENRY FROWDE, M.A.

PUBLISHER TO THE UNIVERSITY OF OXFORD

LONDON, EDINBURGH, AND NEW YORK

THE BOOK OF THE
SECRETS OF ENOCH

FORWARD

Many people assume that *The Book of the Secrets of Enoch* is just another name for the better known *Book of Enoch*. Not true. This book is a completely different work, holding just as much importance on its own as *The Book of Enoch*. It was discovered by the west in 1892 when a German writer announced that a Slavonic version of *The Book of Enoch* existed. It was shortly found and translated by W.R. Morfill, this being that version.

This book is a first hand account by Enoch of his encounter with other-worldly beings who took him from earth and brought him away, up through the "seven heavens." The beings who took him were described as being extremely tall men, as never before seen on earth, whose faces "shone like the sun." They dressed in feathers and had wings that were brighter than gold, and their hands were whiter than snow. These beings may have been the "gods," they may have been angels, or they may have been nothing more than the vivid figments of a dream. But they did make a tremendous impact on Enoch and he was convinced that he'd seen beyond heaven, beyond life, and into another reality.

This became an important holy book for early Christians, then became lost for many centuries thereafter. It is estimated to have been written sometime between 1–50 A.D., and describes Enoch's face to face contact with the Lord Himself after traversing through various heavenly levels. This book is clearly an important research tool in the literature of early Christian thought and religions in general. It is probably the most detailed and important account of a mystical experience that has ever been uncovered from this time period, and therefore deserves to be studied closely. We can learn much from this incredible account.

Paul Tice

PREFACE

—◆—

THE Book of the Secrets of Enoch cannot fail to be of interest to students of Apocalyptic literature and of the origins of Christianity. It is with a view to help such that this the first edition of the book has been undertaken. In certain respects it will appeal also to specialists in Assyriology. So far indeed as it does so, I have been able to do little more than refer to the leading scholars in this department, as my knowledge of such subjects is very slight, and all secondhand.

This book has had a peculiar history. For more than 1200 years it has been unknown save in Russia, where acquaintance with it goes several centuries back. Further, by its present name it was never known in any literature save the Slavonic. Even in Slavonic the name was not quite constant, if we may trust one of the MSS. (B); for there it appears as 'The Secret Books of God which were shown to Enoch.' And yet the book was much read in many circles in the first three centuries of the Church, and has left more traces of its influence than many a well-known book of the same literature (see § 5), and it is undoubtedly of much greater importance in respect of exegesis. In its Greek form it passed current probably under the general designation of Enoch. Occasionally we find that it was not distinguished by those who used it from the older book which has come down to us through the Ethiopic. We have, in fact, in this book another fragmentary survival of the literature that once circulated under the name of Enoch.

That such a book had ever existed was not known in Western Europe till 1892, when a writer in a German review stated that there was a Slavonic version of the Ethiopic Book of Enoch. By Mr. Morfill's help it soon became clear that there was no foundation whatever for such a statement, and subsequent study showed that we had recovered therein an old and valuable pseudepigraph. The next step was naturally to secure its publication, and this was soon made possible through the kindness of the Delegates of the Press.

It will be generally understood that great difficulties beset such an undertaking, and particularly in the case of a book of whose existence there had never been even a surmise in the world of scholarship, and to which there was not a single unmistakable allusion in all ancient literature. The editor in such a case has to pursue untravelled ways, and if, in his efforts to discover the literary environment, the religious views, the date, and language of his author, he has fallen once and again into errors of perception or judgement, he can therein but throw himself on the indulgence of his critics.

The first edition of such a work must have many short-comings. The editor will be grateful for corrections and further elucidations of the text.

In order to appreciate the value of this book in eluci-dating contemporary and subsequent religious thought, the reader should consult pp. xxix–xlvii of the Introduction.

In conclusion, I must express my gratitude to Mr. Morfill for his great kindness in undertaking the translation of the Slavonic texts, and for his unfailing courtesy and unweary-ing energy in the prosecution of the task. It is to him that I am indebted for the account of the Slavonic MSS. in § 2.

R. H. C.

CONTENTS

—◆—

INTRODUCTION

———•———

§ 1. Short Account of the Book.

The Book of the Secrets of Enoch has, so far as is yet
known, been preserved only in Slavonic. It will suit our
convenience to take advantage of this fact, and call it shortly
'the Slavonic Enoch,' in contradistinction to the older book
of Enoch. As the latter has come down to us in its entirety
through the Ethiopic alone, it will be no less convenient to
designate it as 'the Ethiopic Enoch.'

This new fragment of the Enochic literature has only
recently come to light through certain MSS. which were
found in Russia and Servia. My attention was first drawn
to this fact when editing the Ethiopic Enoch by an article by
Kozak on Russian Pseudepigraphic Literature in the *Jahrb.
f. Prot. Theol.* pp. 127–158 (1892). As it was stated in this
article that there was a Slavonic Version of the Book of Enoch
hitherto known through the Ethiopic Version, I at once applied
to Mr. Morfill for help, and in the course of a few weeks we
had before us printed copies of two of the MSS. in question.
It did not take much study to discover that Kozak's statement was absolutely devoid of foundation. The Book of the
Secrets of Enoch was, as it soon transpired, a new pseudepigraph, and not in any sense a version of the older and
well-known Book of Enoch. In many respects it is of no
less value, as we shall see in the sequel.

The Slavonic Enoch in its present form was written some-
where about the beginning of the Christian era.   Its author
or final editor was an Hellenistic Jew, and the place of its
composition was Egypt.

Written at such a date, and in Egypt, it was not to be
expected that it exercised a direct influence on the writers
of the New Testament.   On the other hand, it occasionally
exhibits striking parallelisms in diction and thought, and
some of the dark passages of the latter are all but inexplicable
without its aid.

Although the very knowledge that such a book ever existed
was lost for probably twelve hundred years, it nevertheless
was much used both by Christian and heretic in the early
centuries.   Thus citations appear from it, though without
acknowledgement, in the Book of Adam and Eve, the Apocalypses of Moses and Paul (400–500 A.D.), the Sibylline
Oracles, the Ascension of Isaiah and the Epistle of Barnabas
(70–90 A.D.).   It is quoted by name in the Apocalyptic
portions of the Testaments of Levi, Daniel, and Naphtali
(circ. I A.D.) [1].   It was referred to by Origen and probably
by Clement of Alexandria, and used by Irenaeus, and a few
phrases in the New Testament may be derived from it.

§ 2. The Slavonic Manuscripts.

The Slavonic redaction of the text of the Book of Enoch,
which is now for the first time translated into English, has
come down to us mainly in two versions.   It will be clear
from the evidence in § 4 that they are translations from a lost
Greek original.   The manuscripts may be thus classified.
I. First those in which we find the complete text, and of
these two have been preserved; (*a*) a MS. in the possession

---

[1] The grounds for this date of the
Testaments cannot be stated here,
nor yet for the assumption some pages
later that they sprang from a Hebrew
original. These I hope to give at
length in an edition of these Testaments.

of Mr. A. Khludov; this is a South Russian recension. The MS. belongs to the second half of 'the seventeenth century, and is found in a *Sbornik* or volume of miscellanies containing also lives of the Saints and other religious treatises. This text was published by Mr. A. Popov in the *Transactions of the Historical and Archaeological Society of the University of Moscow*, vol. iii. (Moscow 1880). It is unfortunately in many places very corrupt. It forms the basis of the present text, but where it is corrupt attempts have been made to supply a sounder text from other MSS. It is marked by the letter A in the critical notes to the present translation. (*b*) A MS. discovered by Prof. Sokolov of Moscow in the Public Library of Belgrade in the year 1886. This is a Bulgarian recension, and the orthography belongs to the middle Bulgarian period. This MS. is probably of the sixteenth century. It contains the account of the priesthood of Methuselah and Nir, the birth of Melchizedek and the Deluge. Though this legend does not belong to this Book of Enoch, it is added as an Appendix. II. There is also a shortened and incomplete redaction of the text of which three MSS. are known; (*a*) that preserved in the Public Library of Belgrade; a Serbian redaction, which was printed by Novaković in the sixteenth volume of the literary magazine *Starine* (Agram, 1884). Many of the readings of this MS. are very interesting. It is of the sixteenth century, and is cited as B. (*b*) That in the Vienna Public Library, which is almost identical with the preceding; (*c*) a MS. of the seventeenth century in the possession of Mr. E. Barsov of Moscow.

Of the above MSS. I have direct acquaintance only with A and B: of the other MSS. I have only an indirect knowledge through the text prepared by Prof. Sokolov, which is based on all the above MSS. Unfortunately, however, this text has not fully discriminated these sources. Accordingly, to avoid misconceptions, this text which is designated as *Sok,* is to be understood as representing all authorities other than A and B.

Other fragments of the Book of Enoch are to be found in Tikhonravov's Memorials of Russian Apocryphal Literature (Памятники отреченной русской литературы), and Pypin's Memorials of Old Russian Literature (Памятники старинной русской литературы). By allusions and citations in early Slavonic literature, we can see that these late manuscripts are only copies of much earlier ones, which have perished. Thus Tikhonravov cites from a fourteenth century MS.

The duty of the translator has been a comparatively simple one—to present a text which would be of service to the Western students of apocryphal literature. To this end all philological questions have been subordinated, and therefore my Slavonic friends must not blame me for not going more into linguistic matters. These would be out of place on the present occasion; certainly the time for such a work has not yet come in England. My translation will have served its purpose by enabling my friend, the Rev. R. H. Charles, to treat the subject as fully and learnedly as he has done from the standpoint of Biblical apocryphal literature. In conclusion, I must say that I am glad in however small a way to be able to contribute to such studies through the agency of Mr. Charles. I wish also to express my thanks to Professors Sokolov and Pavlov of the University of Moscow; to the former for allowing me the use of his emendated text and furnishing me with valuable notes on some obscure passages; and to the latter for the kind interest which he has taken in the book.

W. R. M.

§ 3. The Text followed in the Translation.

The formation of the text has been a matter of great difficulty. As I have no knowledge of Slavonic, Mr. Morfill has been so good as to furnish me with literal translations of A, B and of Prof. Sokolov's text. The number of variations

which was unduly great at the outset has to some extent
been diminished by Mr. Morfill's critical acumen. This
careful scholar, however, I should remark, has conscien-
tiously refrained from all but obvious corrections of the text.
Starting then from his translations of the Slavonic MSS.
and of Sokolov's text, I resolved after due examination to
follow A in the main. B of course is followed when it
preserves the obviously better reading, and that it does
frequently. When both A and B are corrupt, I have fallen
back on the text of Sokolov. Occasionally I have been
obliged to follow one reading to the rejection of the others,
in cases where all the readings were equally probable or
improbable. In only two or three passages have I emended
the text, and that in the case of numbers, which are frequently corrupted in tradition through MSS. In all cases
the rejected variants are given in the critical notes below,
so that, in the event of the discovery of fresh critical
materials, the reader can revise the text for himself, and
in the process will reverse, no doubt, many of the editor's
judgements.

As regards the relative merits of A and B, though the
former is very corrupt, it is nevertheless a truer representative
of the original than B. B is really a short *résumé* of the
work—being about half the length of A. In the process of
abbreviation its editor or scribe rejected in some instances
and in others recast entire sections with capricious rearrange-
ments of the text. For an example of the method pursued
occasionally in B the reader can consult the critical notes
on xl.

In A we find many interpolations. Thus in xx. 3 there is
a mention of the tenth heaven, and in xxi–xxii. 3 a description of the eighth, ninth and tenth heavens, though the rest
of the work directly speaks of and indirectly implies only
seven heavens. B omits all reference to this addition in A.
The reader will find many other like additions which have as

a rule been relegated to the critical notes or given in the text in square brackets.

The titles at the head of the chapters are given by A. I have enclosed them in square brackets, as they have no claim to antiquity. They are not given in Sokolov's text, nor are they found in B. A few titles do appear in B, but with one exception these consist merely of *Entry of Enoch into the first heaven, Entry of Enoch into the second heaven,* &c., &c., *Entry of Enoch into the seventh heaven.*

§ 4. The Language and Place of Writing.

1. The main part of this book was written for the first time in Greek. This is shown by such statements, (1) as xxx. 13, 'And I gave him a name (i. e. Adam) from the four substances: the East, the West, the North, and the South.' Adam's name is here derived from the initial letters of the Greek names of the four quarters, i. e. ἀνατολή, δύσις, ἄρκτος, μεσημβρία. This fancy was first elaborated in Greek, as this derivation is impossible in Semitic languages. (2) Again, the writer follows the chronology of the LXX. Enoch is 165 years old when he begat Methuselah. According to the Hebrew and Samaritan chronologies he was 65. Josephus also (*Ant.* i. 3. 3), it is true, adopts the LXX chronology. (3) In l. 4 the writer reproduces the LXX text of Deut. xxxii. 35 against the Hebrew. (4) The writer frequently uses Ecclesiasticus, and often reproduces it almost word for word: cf. xliii. 2, 3—Ecclus. xxiii. 7 ; x. 20, 22, 24: also xlvii. 5— Ecclus. i. 2 : also li. 1, 3—Ecclus. vii. 32 ; ii. 4 : also lxi. 2— Ecclus. xxxix. 25 : also lxv. 2—Ecclus. xvii. 3, 5. (5) lxv. 4 seems to be derived from the Book of Wisdom vii. 17, 18. So far as we can judge, it was the Greek Versions of Ecclesiasticus and Wisdom that our author used.

Some sections of this book were written originally in Hebrew. (See p. xxiv.)

2. This book was written in Egypt, and probably in Alexandria. This is deducible from the following facts. (1) From the variety of speculations which it holds in common with Philo and writings which were Hellenistic in character or circulated largely in Egypt. Thus the existent was created from the non-existent, xxiv. 2; xxv. 1 : cf. Philo, *de Justit.* 7 ; souls were created before the foundation of the world, xxiii. 5: cf. Philo, *de Somno*, i. 22 ; *de Giganti-bus* 3 ; Wisdom viii. 19, 20. Again, man had seven natures or powers, xxx. 9: cf. Philo, *de Mundi Op.* 40. Man could originally see the angels in heaven, xxxi. 2: cf. Philo, *Quaest. in Gen.* xxxii. There is no resurrection of the body, l. 2 ; lxv. 6: so the Book of Wisdom and Philo taught. Finally swearing is reprobated by both, xlix. 1, 2 : cf. Philo, *de Spec. Leg.* ii. 1. (2) The whole Messianic teaching of the Old Testament does not find a single echo in the work of this Hellenized Israelite of Egypt, although he shows familiarity with almost every book of the Old Testament. (3) The Phoenixes and Chalkydries, xii—monstrous serpents with the heads of *crocodiles*—are natural products of the Egyptian imagination. (4) The syncretistic character of the account of the creation, xxv–xxvi, which undoubtedly betrays Egyptian elements.

We should observe further that the arguments that make for a Greek original tend to support the view that the book was written in Egypt, especially when we take them in conjunction with the date of its composition.

§ 5. RELATION OF THE BOOK TO JEWISH AND CHRISTIAN LITERATURE.

The discoveries regarding the planets, &c., which Joel (circ. 1200 A.D.) in his Chronography assigns to Seth are, as we have shown on p. 37, most probably derived ultimately from this Book of Enoch. In like manner the statements regarding the sabbath and the duration of the world, which according to Cedrenus (circ. 1050 A.D.) were drawn from Josephus and the Book of Jubilees are likewise to be assigned to this book; for nothing of this nature appears either in Josephus or the Book of Jubilees. Cedrenus, we should remember, is largely dependent on Syncellus, and Syncellus is very often wrong in his references in the case of Apocalyptic literature (see xxxiii. 1, 2 notes). It is natural that these late writers should err regarding all facts derived from this book, inasmuch as it was already lost to all knowledge many centuries before their day. Let us now pass over these intervening centuries to a time when this book was still in some measure known. Now in the *Book of Adam and Eve* of the fifth century we find two passages drawn from our book which are quotations in sense more than in words. Thus in I. vi we read: 'But the wicked Satan . . . set me at naught, and sought the Godhead, so that I hurled him down from heaven.' This is drawn from xxix. 4, 5: 'One of these in the ranks of the Archangels (i.e. Satan, cf. xxxi. 4) . . . entertained an impossible idea that he should make his throne higher than the clouds over the earth, and should be equal in rank to My power. And I hurled him from the heights.' Again in the *Book of Adam and Eve*, I. viii: 'When we dwelt in the garden . . . we saw his angels that sang praises in heaven.' This comes from xxxi. 2: 'I made for him the heavens open that he should perceive the angels singing the song of triumph.' See notes on xxxi. 2 for similar view in Philo and St. Ephrem. Again in I. xiv of the former book the words: 'The garden, into the abode of light thou longest for, wherein is no darkness,' and I. xi: 'That garden in which was no darkness,' are probably derived from Slav. En. xxxi. 2: 'And there was light without any darkness continually in Paradise.'

Next in the Apocalypse of Moses (ed. Tischend. 1866), p. 19, we have a further development of a statement that appears in our text regarding the sun: see xiv. 2–4 (notes).

In the anonymous writing *De montibus Sina et Sion* 4, we have most probably another trace of the influence of our text in this century. In this treatise the derivation of Adam's name from the initials of the four quarters of the earth is given at length. This derivation appears probably for the first time in literature in xxx. 13 (see note).

In the fourth century there are undoubted indications of its use in the Apocalypse of Paul (ed. Tischend. 1866). Thus the statement, p. 64, οὗτός ἐστιν ὁ παράδεισος, ἔνθα . . . δένδρον παμμεγέθη (sic) ὡραῖον, ἐν ᾧ ἐπανεπαύετο τὸ πνεῦμα τὸ ἅγιον is beyond the possibility of question a Christian adaptation of the Slavonic Enoch viii. 3: 'And in the midst (of Paradise is) the tree of life, in that place, on which God rests, when He comes into Paradise.' Again the words, p. 64, ἐκ τῆς ῥίζης αὐτοῦ ἐξήρχετο . . . ὕδωρ, μεριζόμενον εἰς τέσσαρα ὀρύγματα, and p. 52, ποταμοὶ τέσσαρες . . . ῥέοντες μέλι καὶ γάλα καὶ ἔλαιον καὶ οἶνον, are almost verbal reproductions of our text, viii. 5: 'From its root in the garden there go forth four streams which pour honey and milk, oil and wine, and are separated in four directions.' With two characteristic features of hell in this Apocalypse, i.e. οὐκ ἦν ἐκεῖ φῶς and ὁ πυρινὸς ποταμός (pp. 57, 58), we may compare x. 1 of our text: 'And there was no light there . . . and a fiery river goes forth.'

The peculiar speculation of St. Augustine in the *De Civ.* xxii. 30. 5 seems to be derived ultimately from xxxiii. 2 (see notes). Compare with xxxiii. 2 especially the words: 'Haec tamen septima erit sabbatum nostrum cuius finis non erit vespera, sed dominicus dies velut *octavus aeternus.*'

In the early part of the third and in the second century there is the following evidence of the existence of our text. Thus in the Sibylline Oracles, ii. 75 ὀρφανικοῖς χήραις τ' ἐπιδευομένοις τε παράσχου, and 88 σὴν χεῖρα πενητεύουσιν ὄρεξον are too closely parallel to l. 5—li. 1, 'Stretch out your hands to the orphan, the widow [and the stranger, B om.]. Stretch out your hands to the poor,' to be accidental.

In Irenaeus *contra Haer.* v. 28. 3 we have the Jewish
speculation in our text, xxxiii. 1, 2, reproduced to the effect
that as the work of creation lasted six days so the world
would last 6,000 years, and that there would be 1,000 years
of rest corresponding to the first sabbath after creation.
See text, xxxiii. 1, 2 (notes).

In Origen (according to Methodius ; see Lommatzsch edition,
xxi. p. 59) we find a reference to this speculation : χιλίων γὰρ
ἐτῶν περιοριζομένων εἰς μίαν ἡμέραν ἐν ὀφθαλμοῖς θεοῦ, ἀπὸ τῆς
τοῦ κόσμου γενέσεως μέχρι καταπαύσεως μέχρις ἡμῶν, ὡς οἱ περὶ
τὴν ἀριθμητικὴν φάσκουσι δεινοί, ἐξ ἡμέραι συμπεραιοῦνται.
Ἑξακισχιλιοστὸν ἄρα ἔτος φασὶν ἀπὸ Ἀδὰμ εἰς δεῦρο συντείνειν·
τῇ γὰρ ἑβδομάδι τῷ ἑπτακισχιλιοστῷ ἔτει κρίσιν ἀφίξεσθαί
φασιν.   Whether this passage argues a direct knowledge of
the Slavonic Enoch is doubtful.   There can be no doubt,
however, with regard to the direct reference in the *de Princip.*
i. 3. 2 'Nam et in eo libello ... quem Hermas conscripsit,
ita refertur : Primo omnium crede, quia unus est Deus, qui
omnia creavit atque composuit : qui cum nihil esset prius,
esse fecit omnia. ... Sed et in Enoch libro his similia de-
scribuntur.'   Now since there is no account of the creation
in the Ethiopic Enoch, Origen is here referring to the Slav.
Enoch xxiv–xxx ; xlvii. 3, 4.

The fragment of the Apocalypse of Zephaniah preserved in
Clement, *Strom.* v. 11. 77, is likewise to be traced to our text :
cf. xviii. (notes).

During the years 50–100 A.D. our text seems not to be
without witness in the literature of that period.   Thus in the
Ascension of Isaiah, viii. 16, we read with regard to the angels
of the sixth heaven : 'Omnium una species et gloria aequalis,'
whereas the difference between the angelic orders in the
lower heavens is repeatedly pointed out.   Now in our text,
xix. 1, it is said of the seven bands of angels present in the
sixth heaven that 'there is no difference in their countenances,
or their manner, or the style of their clothing.'

In 4 Ezra [vi. 71] the words 'ut facies eorum luceant sicut sol' are found in i. 5 'Their faces shone like the sun.'

With the Apocalypse of Baruch, iv. 3 'Ostendi eam (i.e. Paradisum) Adamo priusquam peccaret,' compare xxxi. 2.

In the Epistle of Barnabas xv. 4 τί λέγει τό· " συνετέλεσεν ἐν ἐξ ἡμέραις." τοῦτο λέγει ὅτι ἐν ἑξακισχιλίοις ἔτεσιν συντελέσει Κύριος τὰ σύνπαντα. ἡ γὰρ ἡμέρα παρ' αὐτῷ σημαίνει χίλια ἔτη, we have an exposition of the rather confused words in our text, xxxii. 2—xxxiii. In xv. 5-7, however, the writer of this Epistle does not develop logically the thought with regard to the seventh day; for the seventh day on which God rested from His works should in accordance with the same principle of interpretation as in xv. 4 have been taken as a symbol of a thousand years of rest, i.e. the millennium. In xv. 8, how-ever, this writer shows his return to our text by his use of the peculiar phrase 'the eighth day': οὐ τὰ νῦν σάββατα [ἐμοὶ] δεκτά, ἀλλὰ ὃ πεποίηκα, ἐν ᾧ καταπαύσας τὰ πάντα ἀρχὴν ἡμέρας ὀγδόης ποιήσω, ὅ ἐστιν ἄλλου κόσμου ἀρχή. It may not be amiss here to point out that in the next chapter, in verse 5, the Ethiopic Enoch (lxxxix. 56, 66) is quoted as Scripture. The fact, therefore, that Barnabas does not quote our text as Scripture may point to his discrimination between the two books of Enoch to the detriment of the latter. Again in this Epistle, xviii. 1, the words ὁδοὶ δύο εἰσὶν . . . ἥ τε τοῦ φωτὸς καὶ ἡ τοῦ σκότους are derived from our text, xxx. 15, 'I showed him the two ways, the light and the darkness.' Though the Two Ways are often described in early literature (see note on xxx. 15), only in Barnabas are they described in the same terms as in our text.

In the New Testament the similarity of thought and diction is sufficiently large to establish a close connexion, if not a literary dependence. With St. Matt. v. 9, 'Blessed are the peacemakers,' compare lii. 11, 'Blessed is he who establishes peace.' With St. Matt. v. 34, 35, 37, 'Swear not at all: neither by the heaven . . . nor by the earth . . . nor by

Jerusalem, . . . but let your speech be, Yea, yea : Nay, nay,'
compare xlix. 1, 'I will not swear by a single oath, neither
by heaven, nor by earth, nor by any other creature which
God made. . . . If there is no truth in men, let them swear
by a word, yea, yea, or nay, nay.' (See notes.)

With St. Matt. vii. 20, ' By their fruits ye shall know them,'
compare xlii. 14, ' By their works those who have wrought
them are known.' The words ' Be of good cheer, be not afraid,'
St. Matt. xiv. 27, are of frequent occurrence in our text, i. 8 ;
xx. 2 ; xxi. 3, &c. With St. Matt. xxv. 34, ' Inherit the
kingdom prepared for you from the foundation of the world,'
compare ix. 1, 'This place (i.e. Paradise) O Enoch, is prepared for the righteous . . . as an eternal inheritance.' Next
with St. Luke vi. 35 μηδὲν ἀπελπίζοντες, compare xlii. 7, ' Expecting nothing in return ' Next with John xiv. 2, ' In my
Father's house are many mansions,' compare lxi. 2, ' For in
the world to come . . . there are many mansions prepared for
men, good for the good, evil for the evil.' With Acts xiv. 15,
' Ye should turn from these vain things unto the living God,
who made the heaven and the earth,' compare ii. 2, ' Do not
worship vain gods who did not make heaven and earth.' In
the Pauline Epistles there are several parallels in thought
and diction. With Col. i. 16, ' Dominions or principalities
or powers,' compare xx. 1, ' Lordships and principalities and
powers ': with Eph. iv. 25, ' Speak ye truth each one with
his neighbour,' compare xlii. 12, ' Blessed is he in whom
is the truth that he may speak the truth to his neighbour.'
For other Pauline parallels with our text see pp. xxxix–xli.
With Heb. xi. 3, ' The worlds have been framed by the word
of God, so that what is seen hath not been made out of things
which do appear,' compare xxv. 1, ' I commanded . . . that
visible things should come out of invisible,' and xxiv. 2, ' I
will tell thee . . . what things I created from the non-existent,
and what visible things from the invisible.' For two other
parallels of Hebrews with our text see p. xli. With Rev.

i. 16, 'His countenance was as the sun shineth,' compare i. 5, 'Their faces shone like the sun': with ix. 1, 'There was given to him the key of the pit of the abyss,' compare xlii. 1, 'Those who keep the keys and are the guardians of the gates of hell.' With Rev. iv. 6, 'A glassy sea,' compare iii. 3, 'A great sea greater than the earthy sea.' This sea in the first heaven, however, may be merely 'the waters which were above the firmament' (Gen. i. 7). With Rev. x. 5, 6, 'And the angel ... sware ... that there shall be time no longer,' compare lxv. 7, 'Then the times shall perish, and there shall be no year,' &c.: xxxiii. 2, 'Let there be ... a time when there is no computation and no end; neither years, nor months,' &c.

Finally, in the Apocalyptic portions of the Testaments of the XII Patriarchs, which were written probably about the beginning of the Christian era we find our text quoted directly or implied in several instances. In Levi 3 we have an account of the Angels imprisoned in the second heaven: ἐν αὐτῷ εἰσὶ πάντα τὰ πνεύματα τῶν ἐπαγωγῶν εἰς ἐκδίκησιν τῶν ἀνόμων. This must be rendered 'In it are all the spirits of the lawless ones who are kept bound unto (the day of) vengeance.' With this statement compare our text vii. 1, where the fallen angels in the second heaven are described as 'the prisoners suspended, reserved for (and) awaiting the eternal judgement.' Again, in the same chapter of Levi, there are said to be armies in the third heaven, οἱ ταχθέντες εἰς ἡμέραν κρίσεως, ποιῆσαι ἐκδίκησιν ἐν τοῖς πνεύμασι τῆς πλάνης. With these compare the angels of punishment in the third heaven in x. 3. The statement from Enoch in Test. Dan. 5 τῶν πνευμάτων τῆς πλάνης. Ἀνέγνων γὰρ ἐν βίβλῳ Ἐνὼχ τοῦ δικαίου, ὅτι ὁ ἄρχων ὑμῶν ἐστὶν ὁ Σατανᾶς is drawn from xviii. 3, 'These are the Grigori (i.e. Ἐγρηγοροί) who with their prince Satanail rejected the holy Lord.' In the Test. Napth. 4 the authority of Enoch is claimed by the writer as follows: Ἀνέγνων ἐν γραφῇ ἁγίᾳ Ἐνώχ, ὅτι καί γε καὶ ὑμεῖς ἀποστήσεσθε ἀπὸ κυρίου, πορευόμενοι κατὰ πᾶσαν πονηρίαν ἐθνῶν, καὶ ποιήσετε κατὰ πᾶσαν ἀνομίαν

Σοδόμων. καὶ ἐπάξει ὑμῖν κύριος αἰχμαλωσίαν ... ἕως ἂν ἀναλώσῃ κύριος πάντας ὑμᾶς. This is a loose adaptation to later
times of xxxiv. 2, 3, 'And they will fill all the world with
wickedness and iniquity and foul impurities with one another,
sodomy. ... And on this account I will bring a deluge upon
the earth, and I will destroy all.' The quotation in Test.
Sim. 5 is probably derived from the same source, and that in
Test. Benj. 9 ὑπονοῶ δὲ καὶ πράξεις ἐν ὑμῖν οὐ καλὰς ἔσεσθαι,
ἀπὸ λόγων Ἐνὼχ τοῦ δικαίου· πορνεύσετε γὰρ πορνείαν Σοδόμων,
καὶ ἀπώλησθε ἕως βραχύ, may confidently be traced to it.
The words in Test. Juda 18 ἀνέγνων ἐν βίβλοις Ἐνὼχ τοῦ
δικαίου, ὅσα κακὰ ποιήσετε ἐπ' ἐσχάταις ἡμέραις. φυλάξασθε οὖν,
τέκνα μου, ἀπὸ τῆς πορνείας may likewise be founded upon it.
The loose and inaccurate character of the quotations may in
part be accounted for as follows.

Although it is a matter of demonstration that the main
part of the book was written originally in Greek, it seems no
less sure that certain portions of it were founded on Hebrew
originals. Such an hypothesis is necessary owing to the above
Enochic quotations which appear in the Testaments of the XII
Patriarchs. For the fact that the latter work was written in
Hebrew obliges us to conclude that its author or authors
drew upon Hebrew originals in the quotations from Enoch.
I have not attempted in the present work to discriminate
the portions derived from Hebrew originals. For such a task
we have not sufficient materials, and what we have, moreover,
have not been preserved with sufficient accuracy.

§ 6. INTEGRITY AND CRITICAL CONDITION OF THE BOOK.

In its present form this book appears to be derived from one
author. We have in the notes called attention from time to
time to certain inconsistencies, but these may in part be due
to inaccurate tradition; for the book in this respect has
suffered deplorably. There are of course occasional interpo-

lations—of these some are Jewish, and one or two are
Christian : xxxvii seems foreign to the entire text.

The text, further, has suffered from disarrangement. Thus
xxviii. 5 should be read after xxix, and, together with that
chapter, should be restored before xxviii.

§ 7. DATE AND AUTHORSHIP.

The question of the date has to a large extent been determined already. The portions which have a Hebrew background are at latest pre-Christian. This follows from the
fact of their quotation in the Testaments of the XII Patriarchs.
As I have remarked above (p. xxiv) it is impossible to
define the exact extent of such sections.

Turning, therefore, to the date of the rest of the book, we
can with tolerable certainty discover the probable limits of its
composition. The earlier limit is determined by the already
existing books from which our author has borrowed. Thus
Ecclesiasticus is frequently drawn upon : see xliii. 2, 3 (notes);
xlvii. 5 (note) ; lii. 8 (note); lxi. 2, 4 (notes), &c. The Book of
Wisdom also seems to have been laid under contribution : see
lxv. 4 (note). With this book our author shares certain closely
related Hellenistic views. Again, as regards the Ethiopic
Enoch, our author at times reproduces the phraseology and
conceptions of that book : see vii. 4, 5 (notes) ; xxxiii. 4
(note), 9, 10 (notes); xxxv. 2 (note), &c. ; at others he gives
the views of the former in a developed form : see viii. 1, 5, 6
(notes) ; xl. 13 (note); lxiv. 5 ; at others he enunciates views
which are absolutely divergent from the former : see xvi. 7
(note) ; xviii. 4 (note). It is noteworthy also that our author
claims to have explained certain natural phenomena, but the
explanations in question are not to be found in his writings
but in the Ethiopic Enoch : see xl. 5, 6, 8, 9 (notes). Finally
we observe the same advanced view on Demonology appearing
in the Slavonic Enoch and in the latest interpolation in the
Ethiopic Enoch ; see xviii. 3 (note).

Ecclesiasticus, the Book of Wisdom (?), and the Ethiopic
Enoch (in its latest and present form) were thus at our
author's service. The earlier limit of composition, accordingly,
lies probably between 30 B. C. and the Christian era.

We have now to determine the later limit. This must
be set down as earlier than 70 A. D. For, (1) the temple is
still standing; see lix. 2 (notes). (2) Our text was probably
known to some of the writers of the New Testament (see
pp. xxi–xxiii; xxxix–xliii). (3) It was known and used by
the writers of the Epistle of Barnabas and of the latter half
of the Ascension of Isaiah.

We may, therefore, with reasonable certainty assign the
composition of our text to the period 1–50 A. D. The date of
the Hebrew original underlying certain sections of our text is
as we have already seen pre-Christian.

The author was a Jew who lived in Egypt, probably in
Alexandria. He belonged to the orthodox Hellenistic Judaism
of his day. Thus he believed in the value of sacrifices, xlii.
6; lix. 1, 2; lxvi. 2; but he is careful to enforce enlightened
views regarding them, xlv. 3, 4; lxi. 4, 5; in the law, lii.
8, 9; and likewise in a blessed immortality, l. 2; lxv. 6,
8–10; in which the righteous shall wear 'the raiment of
God's glory,' xxii. 8. In questions affecting the origin of
the earth, sin, death, &c., he allows himself the most unre-
stricted freedom and borrows freely from every quarter. Thus,
Platonic (xxx. 16, note), Egyptian (xxv. 2, note), and Zend
(lviii. 4–6 notes) elements are adopted into his system. The
result is naturally syncretistic.

The date (1–50 A. D.) thus determined above makes our
author a contemporary of Philo. We have shown above
(p. xvii) that they share many speculations in common, but in
some they are opposed. Thus our author protests against the
Jewish belief in the value of the intercession of departed
saints for the living; see liii. 1 (note). Philo undoubtedly
taught this, *De Exsecrat.* 9.

§ 8. Some of the Author's views on Creation, Anthropology, and Ethics.

God in the beginning created the world out of nothing, xxiv. 2 [1]. (For a detailed account of each day's creations see xxv-xxx.) In this creation He made seven heavens, xxx. 2, 3 [2], and all the angelic hosts—the latter were created on the first day—and all animal and plant life, and finally man on the sixth day. After His work on the six days God rested on the seventh. These six days of work followed by a seventh of rest are at once a history of the past and a forecasting of the future. As the world was made in six days, so its history would be accomplished in 6,000 years, and as the six days of creation were followed by one of rest, so the 6,000 years of the world's history would be followed by a rest of 1,000 years, i. e. the millennium [3]. On its close would begin the eighth eternal day of blessedness when time should be no more, xxxii. 2—xxxiii. 2.

As regards man, all the souls of men were created before the foundation of the world, xxiii. 5, and also a future place of abode in heaven or hell for every individual soul, xlix. 2 ; lviii. 5 ; lxi. 2. The world was made for man's sake, lxv. 3. When Wisdom made man of seven substances, xxx. 8, at God's command, God gave him the name Adam from the four quarters of the earth—ἀνατολή, δύσις, ἄρκτος, μεσημβρία —xxx. 13. Man's soul was created originally good, while in the garden he could see the angels in heaven, xxxi. 2. Free-will was bestowed upon him, and the knowledge of good and evil. He was likewise instructed in the Two Ways of light and darkness, and then left to mould his own destiny, xxx. 15.

[1] Or else formed it out of pre-existing elements, xxv. 1, where we have an adaptation of the egg theory of the universe.

[2] Hell was in the north of the third heaven. It is possible, however, that there were also seven hells; see xl. 12 (note).

[3] This millennium seems to be identical with a Messianic age, xxxv. 3 (note).

But the incorporation of the soul in the body with its necessary limitations biassed its preferences in the direction of evil, and death came in as the fruit of sin, xxx. 16. Men and angels will be judged and punished for every form of sin [1], xl. 12, 13; xlvi. 3; lxv. 6; but the righteous will escape the last judgement, lxv. 8; lxvi. 7; and will be gathered in eternal life, lxv. 8, and will be seven times brighter than the sun, lxvi. 7, and they will have no labour, nor sickness, nor sorrow, nor anxiety, nor need, and an incorruptible paradise shall be their protection and their eternal habitation, lxv. 9, 10. As for sinners there is no place of repentance after death, xlii. 2, but hell is prepared for them as an eternal inheritance, x. 4, 6. And there is no intercession of departed saints for the living, liii. 1.

In an ethical regard there are many noble sentiments to be found in our author, but generally in a very unliterary form. The Slavonic Version is, no doubt, partially to be blamed here. I will append here an outline of a man's ethical duties with sundry beatitudes according to our author. Every man should work; for blessed is he who looks to raise his own hand for labour, but cursed is he who looks to make use of another man's labour, lii. 7, 8. And men, likewise, should be unselfishly just; for blessed is he who executes a just judgement, not for the sake of recompense, but for the sake of righteousness, expecting nothing in return, xlii. 7. And men should also practice charity and beneficence. They should not hide their silver in the earth, but assist the honest man in his affliction, li. 2, and stretch out their hands to the orphan, the widow and the stranger, l. 5, and give bread to the hungry, and clothe the naked, and raise the fallen, and walk without blame before the face of the Lord, ix. Furthermore, men should not swear either by heaven or earth or by any other creature which God made, but by a word, yea, yea, or nay, nay,

---

[1] Observe that men will be specially punished for ill-treatment of animals, lviii. 4-6.

xlix. 1 ; neither should they avenge themselves, l. 4, nor abuse
and calumniate their neighbour, lii. 2 ; but endure every
affliction and every evil word and attack for the sake of the
Lord, l. 3 ; li. 3. Moreover, they should shun pride : for God
hates the proud, lxiii. 4; and walk in long-suffering, in humility,
in faith and truth, in sickness, in abuse, in temptation, in
nakedness, in deprivation, loving one another till they depart
from this world of sickness, lxvi. 6. Finally, whereas one man
is more honourable than another, either on the ground of
cunning or of strength, of purity or wisdom, of comeliness or
understanding, let it be heard everywhere that none is greater
than he who fears God, xliii. 2, 3.

§ 9. The Value of this Book in elucidating contemporary and subsequent Religious Thought.

On the value of this book in elucidating contemporary and
subsequent religious thought I shall be brief, save in the case
of the doctrine of the seven heavens. This doctrine is set
forth by our author with a fullness and clearness not found
elsewhere in literature. Thus many gaps in our knowledge of
this doctrine have been filled up. It will not be surprising,
therefore, if we are thus enabled to explain certain mysterious
allusions bearing on this conception in the Bible and elsewhere, which have hitherto been doubtful or inexplicable.

Some of the beliefs which appear in our text, and which in
some instances are either partially or wholly elucidated, are
as follows :

1. *Death was caused by Sin.* This was a comparatively late
view : see notes on pp. 43, 44.

2. *The millennium.* This Jewish conception is first found in
this book, xxxii. 2—xxxiii. 2, and the rationale of its origin is
clear from this passage when taken together with statements on
the same subject in later writers (see notes *in loc.*, and p. xxvii).
Its origin was as follows. The account in Genesis of the first
week of creation came in pre-Christian times to be regarded

not only as a history of the past, but as a forecast of the future
history of the world so created. Thus as the world was created
in six days, so its history was to be accomplished in 6,000
years ; for 1,000 years are with God as one day (cf. Ps. xc. 4 ;
Jub. iv. 30 ; 2 Pet. iii. 8 ; Barnabas, *Ep.* xiv. 4 ; Iren. *contra
Haer.* v. 28. 2 ; Justin M., *Dial. c. Tryph.* 80), and as God
rested on the seventh day, so at the close of the 6,000 years
there would be a rest of 1,000 years, i. e. the millennium.

3. *On the creation of man with freewill and the knowledge of
good and evil,* see xxx. 15 (notes).

4. *The Seraphim.* In the Chalkidri [1], xii. 1, we have in all
probability the serpents who are mentioned in the Ethiopic
Enoch xx. 7 along with the Cherubim. They are a class of
heavenly creatures, and like the Cherubim are formed by
a combination of the members of different animals. The
serpent-like form, however, predominated, and hence they were
δρακόντες in Greek (Eth. En. xx. 7), and Seraphim (שרפים) in
Hebrew. How the peculiar name Chalkidri (= Χαλκύδραι
brazen serpents ?) arose I cannot say, as it is by no means
appropriate. The main objection to identifying the Chalkidri
with the Seraphim of the Old Testament is the fact that our
author only mentions them here in connexion with the sun,
xii. 1 ; xv. 1 ; and speaks directly of Seraphim elsewhere,
xx. 1. However this may be, the passage in the Eth. Enoch
xx. 7 is conclusive as to the serpent-like forms of the Seraphim.
By this interpretation the word receives the meaning which it
naturally has in the Hebrew.

5. *On the intercession of Saints,* see liii. 1 (note).

6. *The seven Heavens—an early Jewish and Christian belief.*

Various conceptions of the seven heavens prevailed largely
in the ancient world, alike in the far east and in the west.
With these we shall deal only in so far as they influenced
or were in any degree akin to the views that prevailed on this
subject among the Jews and early Christians.

---

[1] Variously spelt in the MSS. as Chalkadri, Chalkidri, Chalkedry.

For the sake of clearness it may be well to indicate the direction our investigations will take. We shall first set forth or merely mention the beliefs of this nature that prevailed among the Babylonians and the followers of Zoroaster in the East and the speculations of certain Greek philosophers in the West. We shall next touch briefly on certain indications in the Old Testament that point in the direction of a plurality of the heavens, and show that Israel was not unaffected by the prevailing traditions of the ancient world.

That we have not misinterpreted such phenomena in the Old Testament, we are assured, when we descend to Jewish Apocalyptic writings, such as the Testaments of the XII Patriarchs, the Slavonic Enoch, 4 Ezra, and to the Talmud, and the Mandaic Religion. Having thus shown that speculations or definitely formulated views on the plurality of the heavens were rife in the very cradle of Christendom and throughout its entire environment, we have next to consider whether Christian conceptions of heaven were shaped or in any degree modified by already existing ideas on this subject. We shall find that there is undoubted evidence of the belief in the plurality or sevenfold division of the heavens in the Pauline Epistles, in Hebrews, and in the Apocalypse.

In early Christian literature such ideas soon gained clearer utterance in Christian Apocalypses, such as the Ascension of Isaiah, the Apocalypses of Moses, Ezra, John, Isaac, Jacob, and the Acts of Callistratus. Such writers also as Clement of Alexandria and Origen are more or less favourably inclined to such conceptions. But shortly after this date these views fell into the background, discredited undoubtedly by the exaggerations and imbecilities with which they were accompanied. And thus though a Philastrius declares disbelief in a plurality of the heavens a heresy, Chrysostom is so violently affected against such a conception that he denies any such plurality at all. Finally such conceptions, failing in the course of the next few centuries to find a home in Christian lands, betook themselves to Mohammedan countries, where they found a ready welcome and a place of authority in the temple of Moslem theology. We shall now proceed as we have above indicated.

Among the Babylonians we find that hell was divided into seven parts by seven concentric walls (see Sayce, *Babylonian Religion*, 1887, pp. 221-227; Jensen, *Die Kosmologie der Babylonier*, Strasburg, 1890, pp. 232-3[1]). Hence, we may here observe, this view passed over into the Talmud (Feuchtwang, *Zeitschr. f. Assyr.*, iv. 42, 43).

This sevenfold division of things in general was a familiar one among this people[2]. Thus the cities, Erech and Ecbatana, were each surrounded by seven walls, modelled, no doubt, as Jensen conjectures, on their conception of the seven worldzones (*op. cit.* 172). For the world was held to be divided in this fashion according to the *Gudia* (*op. cit.* 173). This division was due either to the overwhelming importance of the sacred number seven, or else specifically to the number of the planets (*op. cit.* 174). We should observe also that the temple of Erech was called the temple of the seven divisions. Since, therefore, both earth and hell were divided into seven zones, it is only reasonable to infer that a similar conception was entertained regarding the heavens. Jensen, indeed, says that he can find no trace of such a division in the inscriptions. But since the sevenfold division of the planets gave birth to the sevenfold division of earth and hell, it is next to impossible to avoid the inference with Sayce and Jeremias that this same division must have been applied to the heavens through which the planets moved.

In Parseeism we find the doctrine of the seven heavens. This does not appear in the earliest writings, but in the Ardâi-virâf-nâme there is an account of the seven heavens

---

[1] See also Jeremias, *Die babyl.-assur. Vorstellungen vom Leben nach dem Tode*, 1887, pp. 34-45.

[2] Cf. Sayce, *Babylonian Religion*, p. 82 note.

through which Sosiash made a progress in seven days.   In the first heaven are men who feel heat and cold simultaneously. (If we might infer from corresponding ideas in the Slavonic Enoch, and other apocalypses, we should conclude this heaven to be an abode of the wicked, and not of the good.   There is, however, a hell independently of this.)   The inhabitants of the second heaven shine as the stars; of the third as the moon ; of the fourth as the sun.   The blessedness of endless light is reserved for heroes, lawgivers, and the preeminently pious.   In the seventh heaven Zarathustra sits on a golden throne.   As we have already remarked, there is only one hell mentioned in the Ardâi-virâf-nâme.   On the influence which such ideas had on the Talmud see Kohut, *Zeitschrift D M G,* xxi. 562.

If we now turn from the East to the West, we meet first of all with the Pythagorean tenfold division of the universe. In the centre there was the central fire around which revolved from west to east the ten heavenly bodies.   Furthest off was the heaven of fixed stars ; next came the five planets ; then the sun, the moon, the earth, and finally the counter earth [1].   According to the *Timaeus* of Plato the universe is shaped as a sphere at the centre of which is placed the earth. Next follow the sun, the moon, and the five other planets, revolving round the earth in orbits separated from each other by distances corresponding to the intervals of the harmonic system.   The outermost circle is formed of the heaven of fixed stars.

When we turn to the Stoics we find kindred conceptions ; in the centre of the universe the earth is placed in a state of repose.   Nearest to the earth revolves the moon, and next in their appropriate orbits the Sun, Venus, Mercury, Mars, Jupiter, Saturn.

We have thus seen that speculations were rife throughout

---

[1] For further details see the English translation of Zeller's *Pre-Socratic Philosophy,* i. 444–5.

the ancient world on the plurality of the heavens. It is clear further that these speculations were based mainly on astronomical considerations. That ancient Judaism was not unaffected by such views we may reasonably conclude from certain passages in the Old Testament. The plural form of the word for 'heaven' in Hebrew probably points to a plurality of heavens. Such phrases as 'the heaven of heavens,' Deut. x. 14; 1 Kings viii. 27; Ps. cxlviii. 4, cannot be adequately interpreted unless in reference to such a belief. In Job i. 6, 7 ; ii. 1, 2, 7 we find a further peculiar feature in the ancient conception of heaven. Satan there presents himself along with the angels in the presence of God. The place indicated by the context is heaven. Similarly in 1 Kings xxii. 19–22 an evil spirit presents himself among the heavenly hosts before the throne of God. The presence of evil in heaven, though offensive to the conscience of later times, seems to have caused no offence in early Semitic thought.

We shall find in the course of our investigations that this peculiar idea reasserted itself from time to time in Judaism and Christianity till finally it was expelled from both.

The probability of an Old Testament belief in the plurality of the heavens is heightened, if we consider the fact that the Jews were familiar with and attached names to the planets. Thus Kronos, Aphrodite, Ares, Zeus, Hermes are mentioned respectively in Amos v. 26 ; Is. xiv. 12; 2 Kings xvii. 30 ; Is. lxv. 11 ; xlvi. 1. The Jews were acquainted also with the signs of the Zodiac (Job xxxviii. 32), and offered them an idolatrous worship (2 Kings xxiii. 5).

Since, therefore, we have seen that in the East astronomical considerations, i. e. the sevenfold division of the planets led in due course to a similar division of the heavens, it is not unlikely that this knowledge gave birth to a like result among the Jews.

However this may be, the reasonable probability we have

already arrived at is converted into a certainty when we come down to the Apocalyptic and other writings of the Jews. Of these, the Slavonic Enoch and the Apocalyptic sections of the Testaments of the XII Patriarchs were written about or before the beginning of the Christian Era. As the description of the seven heavens in the latter is very brief we shall deal with it first. The rendering that follows presupposes an emendation of Dr. Sinker's text, which I cannot justify here, but hope to do so later in an edition of this work.

The third chapter of the Testament of Levi runs: ' Hear then concerning the seven heavens. The lowest is the gloomiest, because it witnesses every iniquity of men. The second has fire, snow, ice, ready against the day of the ordinance of the Lord, in the righteous judgement of God. In it are all the spirits of the lawless ones which are confined for punishment. (Cf. Slav. Enoch vii.) In the third are the hosts of the armies (cf. Slav. Enoch xvii) which are appointed against the day of judgement to execute vengeance on the spirits of deceit and of Beliar. . . . In the highest of all the Great Glory dwells, in the holy of holies. . . . In the heaven next to it (i. e. the sixth) are the angels of the presence of the Lord, who minister and make propitiation to the Lord for all the sins of ignorance of the righteous. . . . And in the heaven below this (i. e. the fifth) are the angels who bear the answers to the angels of the presence of the Lord. And in the heaven next to this (i. e. the fourth) are thrones, authorities, in which hymns are ever offered to God.' In chapter ii of the same Testament there is a short reference to the first three heavens: ' And I entered from the first heaven into the second, and I saw there water hanging between the two. And I saw a third heaven brighter than these two.'

We cannot pause here to deal with the details of the above account. We shall only draw attention to the description of the denizens of the second heaven. These are the fallen angels who are reserved for punishment. Although the description of the seven heavens just given is short, it is too definitely conceived to have appeared thus for the first time in Judaism. In the Slavonic Enoch, whose evidence we shall presently briefly summarize, we have, so far as I am aware, the most elaborate account of the seven heavens that exists in any writing or in any language. 'The Book of the Secrets of Enoch,' as it is named in the Slavonic MSS. in which it is alone preserved, but which for the sake of brevity I call 'the Slavonic Enoch,' was written in the main in Greek, at Alexandria, although portions of it are merely reproductions of a Hebrew original. In the first heaven there is 'a very great sea, greater than any earthly sea.' (Cf. Rev. iv. 6.) This sea seems to be described in the Testaments of the XII Patriarchs as 'water hanging between the first and second heavens.' (See above.) In this heaven also are 'the elders and the rulers of the orders of the stars.' Although the number of these is not given, it is either twelve (and then we have here an account related to Eth. En. lxxxii. 9–18, 20) or possibly it is twenty-four, and thus there may be a remote connexion on the one hand between this class of 'elders and rulers . . . of the stars' and the twenty-four elders in Rev. iv. 4, and on the other between it and the Babylonian idea set forth in Diodorus Siculus, ii. 31 μετὰ δὲ τὸν ζῳδιακὸν κύκλον εἴκοσιν καὶ τέτταρας ἀφορίζουσιν ἀστέρας, ὧν τοὺς μὲν ἡμίσεις ἐν τοῖς βορείοις μέρεσι, τοὺς δὲ ἡμίσεις ἐν τοῖς νοτίοις τετάχθαι φασί, καὶ τούτων τοὺς μὲν ὁρωμένους τῶν ζώντων εἶναι καταριθμοῦσι, τοὺς δ' ἀφανεῖς τοῖς τετελευτηκόσι προσωρίσθαι νομίζουσιν, οὓς δικαστὰς τῶν ὅλων προσαγορεύουσιν (quoted by Gunkel, *Schöpfung und Chaos,* p. 308, who establishes a connexion between Rev. iv. 4 and this Babylonian idea). The first heaven, further, contains treasuries of snow, ice, clouds, and dew.

In the second heaven (chap. vii) Enoch saw the prisoners suspended reserved for and awaiting the eternal judgement. 'And these angels were gloomy in appearance, . . . they had apostatized from the Lord and transgressed together with their prince.' For a similar account see Test. Levi, above.

In the third heaven (chap. viii) we have the garden of Eden and the tree of life, and likewise 'an olive tree always distilling oil,' i. e. the *arbor misericordiae* (cf. Evang. Nicodemi, ii. 3). We should observe that the location of Paradise in this heaven agrees with the Pauline account 2 Cor. xii. 2, 3.

But (chap. x) in the northern region of this heaven Enoch sees the place of the damned. 'That place has fire on all sides and on all sides cold and ice, thus it burns and freezes.' When Enoch exclaims, 'Woe, woe! how terrible is this place!' his escort replies: 'This place, Enoch, is prepared for those who did not honour God; who commit evil deeds on earth, sodomy, witchcraft, enchantments, . . . stealing, lying, calumnies, envy, evil thoughts, fornication, murder. (Chap. x. 4.)

In the fourth heaven (chap. xi–xv) Enoch sees the course of the sun and moon, and the angels and the wonderful creatures, the phoenixes and the chalkidri, which wait upon the sun. In the midst of this heaven (chap. xvii) are 'the armed host serving the Lord with cymbals and organs and unceasing voice.' Cf. Test. Levi on third and fourth heavens above.

In the fifth heaven (chap. xviii) are the watchers whose fallen brethren Enoch had already seen undergoing torments in the second heaven. These are troubled and silent on account of their brethren.

In the sixth heaven (chap. xix) are 'seven bands of angels, very bright and glorious,' who arrange and study the revolutions of the stars and the changes of the moon and the revolutions of the sun, &c.; 'And the angels over all the souls of men who write down all their works and their lives before the face of the Lord. In their midst are seven phoenixes and seven cherubim and seven six-winged creatures.'

In the seventh heaven (chap. xx) Enoch sees all the heavenly hosts, the ten great orders of angels standing before the Lord in the order of their rank, and the Lord sitting on His lofty throne.

With regard to this scheme, I will content myself with calling attention to the fact that a preliminary Tartarus is situated in the second heaven (cf. second heaven in the Test. Levi); and that hell is placed in the north of the third heaven, and that evil in various forms is found in the second and third heavens, and dissatisfaction and trouble in the fifth.

In 4 Ezra (vi. 55–74) there is a detailed description of the seven ways of the wicked and the seven ways of the righteous. These ways are represented in a form so essentially abstract, that as Gunkel rightly remarks (*op. cit.* p. 309), they must be derived from what were originally concrete conceptions such as the seven heavens and the seven hells. To the latter conception there is no reference in the Slavonic Enoch : yet see xl. 12 (note).

Passing onward we come to the Talmud. In the Talmud the views of the Rabbis waver. Some thought as the Rabbi Jehuda that there were two heavens, *Chagiga* 12^b, but Rabbi Simeon ben Lakish enumerated seven. This latter view was the usual one. In the *Beresh. rabba* c. 6 and the *Chagiga* 12^b, the seven heavens are as follows. The lowest which is called *vilun* is empty. In the second, named *rakía*, are the sun, moon, and stars. In the third, named *shechaqim*, are the mills which grind the manna for the righteous. In the fourth heaven, *zebul*, are the heavenly Jerusalem, the temple, the altar, and Michael. In the fifth, *maon*, are the angels who sing by night, but are silent by day in order that God may hear the praises of Israel. In the sixth, *machon*, are the treasuries of the snow, hail, rain, and dew. In the seventh, *aravoth*, are judgement and righteousness, the treasures of life, peace, and blessing, the souls of the departed pious as

well as the spirits and souls yet to be born, and the dew
wherewith God will awake the dead. Finally there are the
seraphim, ophannim, chayyoth and other angels of service,
and God Himself sitting on a throne. See Weber, *Die Lehren
des Talmud,* pp. 197–8; Eisenmenger, *Entdecktes Judenthum,*
i. 467; Wetstein on 2 Cor. xii.

It is well to observe here that, though the Talmudic
description of the seven heavens is puerile in the extreme,
its character attests the influence of a growing ethical consciousness.

To such a consciousness the presence of evil in heaven
could not but seem incongruous. In banishing evil, however,
from the precincts of the heavens, the Rabbis weakened the
vigour of the old conceptions; for they were not masters of
sufficient imagination to fill up adequately the gaps brought
about by their righteous zeal. In connexion with Jewish
evidence on this subject, we might point out that the same
division of the heavens probably prevailed in the Mandaic
Religion, since at all events one of its dogmas was the
sevenfold division of hell (Brandt, *Die Mandäische Religion,*
p. 182).

We have now found that among the Babylonians, the
later followers of Zoroaster, the Greeks, in all probability in
ancient Judaism, and certainly in Judaism generally from
before the Christian Era onward, speculations, and as a rule
clearly defined conceptions, were rife on the plurality of the
heavens. We have seen also that the prevailing view was
that of the sevenfold division of the heavens, and we have
observed further that a feature impossible in modern conceptions of heaven shows itself from time to time in pre-
Christian religious conceptions, i.e. the belief in the presence
of evil in the heavens.

We have now to consider whether Christian conceptions
of heaven were shaped, or in any degree influenced, by already
existing views of that nature. A knowledge of ancient

thought on this subject would naturally lead us to expect such an influence at work, and we find on examination that our expectations are in certain respects fully realized. First from 2 Cor. xii. 2, 3 we learn that St. Paul believed in a plurality of the heavens. 'I know a man in Christ fourteen years ago . . . such a one caught up even to the third heaven. And I know such a man . . . how that he was caught up into Paradise.'

Heretofore exegetes have been divided as to whether St. Paul believed in the existence of three heavens or of seven. Owing to the fresh evidence on the subject furnished by the Slavonic Enoch there is no longer room for reasonable doubt on the question.   In the Slavonic Enoch we have presented to us a scheme of the seven heavens which in some of its prominent features agrees with that conceived by St. Paul. Thus in the Slavonic Enoch Paradise is situated in the third heaven as in 2 Cor. xii. 2, 3, whereas according to later Judaism it belonged to the fourth heaven (see above).   In the next place the presence of evil in some part of the heavens is recognized. Thus in Eph. vi. 12 we meet with the peculiar statement 'Against the spiritual hosts of wickedness in the heavens,' πρὸς τὰ πνευματικὰ τῆς πονηρίας ἐν τοῖς ἐπουρανίοις. The phrase ἐν τοῖς ἐπουρανίοις occurs only in Ephesians of the Pauline Epistles. It is found five times i. 3, 20; ii. 6; iii. 10; and vi. 12, and always in a local sense. It is thus in fact = ἐν τοῖς οὐρανοῖς.

This phrase is then capable of two interpretations. The 'hosts' in question are the fallen angels in the second heaven, or else the powers of Satan, the prince of the air (cf. Eph. ii. 2).   For the latter interpretation the Slavonic Enoch xxix. 4, 5 might be quoted as a parallel: 'One of the ranks of the archangels, having turned away with the rank below him, entertained an impossible idea, that he should make his throne higher than the clouds over the earth, and should be equal in rank to My power. And I hurled him from the heights with his angels. And he was flying in the air continually above the abyss.' The latter explanation of ἐν τοῖς ἐπουρανίοις is probably right. In Col. i. 20, however, we must, if we deal honestly with the context, suppose some such a view of the heavens as that given in the Slavonic Enoch to underlie the words: 'To reconcile all things unto Himself, whether things upon the earth or things in the heavens.' That 'things upon earth' need to be reconciled to God is universally intelligible; but so far as I am aware no exegete has hitherto recognized any such necessity on the part of 'things in the heavens.' Yet this is the obvious meaning of the words. Hence 'the things in the heavens' that are to be reconciled to God must be either the fallen angels imprisoned in the second heaven, or else the powers of Satan whose domain is the air. Though to some universalistic aspects of Paulinism the conversion of Satan is not impossible, it is nevertheless unlikely to be his thought here. Hence we seem to be restricted to the other interpretation, and thus we have therein an indirect parallel to 1 Pet. iii. 19, 'He went and preached to the spirits in prison.' Another statement in Eph. iii. 10 belongs to the same plane of thought: 'To the intent that now unto the principalities and the powers in the heavens (ἐν τοῖς ἐπουρανίοις) might be made known through the church the manifold wisdom of God.' These 'principalities and powers' may also be taken as the fallen angels in the second heaven; but it is more likely that they are the rulers of the various lower heavens which are mentioned in iv. 10: 'He . . . that ascended far above all the heavens.' This thought of the seven heavens through which Christ passed or above which he was exalted twice recurs in Hebrews iv. 14: 'Having then a great high priest, who hath passed through the heavens' (διεληλυθότα τοὺς οὐρανούς); vii. 26: 'Made higher than the heavens' (ὑψηλότερος τῶν οὐρανῶν γενόμενος). Before we pass on to the consideration of the Apocalypse, we should observe that Paul used οὐρανός [1] frequently (cf. Rom. i. 18 ; x. 6 ; 1 Cor. viii. 5 ; xv. 47), though he believed in a plurality of the heavens.

In the twelfth chapter of Revelation we have a record of the war in heaven between Michael and his angels against Satan and his angels, with the subsequent overthrow and expulsion of the latter. These events spiritually interpreted symbolize, it is true, the victory of good over evil, but when studied in reference to their origin, they mark a revolutionizing of the old Semitic conception of heaven. Evil can no longer be conceived as possible in the abode of righteousness, nor can its place be any more found in heaven. And thus Satan and his angels are cast down to the earth. When once evil in all its forms is driven forth from heaven, the rationale of a sevenfold division of it disappears. There are then no longer conflicting elements which must be restricted to certain divisions and kept apart by concrete barriers. The old Semitic doctrine of the seven heavens really presupposes in some respects dualistic influences. Such a conception could not long hold its ground in a monistic faith. It was this dualistic tinge that made it so acceptable with the heretics. We must now follow the subsequent fortunes of this doctrine in the early centuries of Christianity.

First we find in one of the Christian sections (chaps. vi–xi) of the Ascension of Isaiah an elaborate but sinewless account of the seven heavens. Evil has already been expelled, and the inhabitants of one heaven differ from those of another merely in possessing greater degrees of glory and knowledge. This account of the seven heavens is singularly wanting in variety and imaginative power : it is valuable, however, in an historical reference.

---

[1] The singular and plural of this word are used, according to Sir J. C. Hawkins, in the New Testament as follows :—

	Mat.	Mark	Luke	John	Acts	Paul.	Heb.	James	Pet.	Rev.
οὐρανός	27	12	31	18	24	11	3	2	1	51
οὐρανοί	55	5	4	0	2	10	7	0	5	1*

*xii. 12—a quotation from, or reference to Is. xliv. 23 and xlix. 13.

Leaving the Ascension of Isaiah, we shall now give the evidence of Clement of Alexandria and Origen on the prevalence of this doctrine.

In the *Stromata* iv. 25 of Clement there is a reference to the seven heavens which are obviously regarded as a true conception ; while in v. 11 we have a quotation from a lost Apocalypse of Zephaniah : ἆρ᾽ οὐχ ὅμοια ταῦτα τοῖς ὑπὸ Σοφονία λεχθεῖσι τοῦ προφήτου; καὶ ἀνέλαβέν με πνεῦμα καὶ ἀνήνεγκέν με ὡς οὐρανὸν πέμπτον καὶ ἐθεώρουν ἀγγέλους καλουμένους κυρίους . . . ὑμνοῦντας θεὸν ἄρρητον ὕψιστον.

This passage seems to be ultimately derived from the Slavonic Enoch xviii.

In the lost Book of Baruch the Prophet, there was some account of the seven heavens according to Origen, *de Princip.* ii. 3, 6 : ʻDenique etiam Baruch prophetae librum in assertionis huius testimonium vocant, quod ibi de septem mundis vel coelis evidentius indicatur.ʼ

But to proceed to Origen's own views we read in *contra Cels.* vi. 21 as follows : ἑπτὰ δὲ οὐρανούς, ἢ ὅλως περιωρισμένον ἀριθμὸν αὐτῶν, αἱ φερόμεναι ἐν ταῖς ἐκκλησίαις τοῦ θεοῦ οὐκ ἀπαγγέλλουσι γραφαί· ἀλλ᾽ οὐρανούς, εἴτε τὰς σφαίρας τῶν παρ᾽ Ἕλλησι λεγομένων πλανήτων, εἴτε καὶ ἄλλο τι ἀπορρητότερον ἐοίκασι διδάσκειν οἱ λόγοι.

Though Origen says that there is no authoritative teaching as to there being seven heavens, it is clear that he really believes in there being this number ; for elsewhere he identifies these heavens with the planets of the Greeks, *de Princip.* ii. 11. 6 : ʻ Si quis sane mundus corde, et purior mente, et exercitatior sensu fuerit, velocius proficiens cito ad aeris locum adscendet, et ad coelorum regna perveniet per locorum singulorum, ut ita dixerim, mansiones, quas Graeci quidem sphaeras, id est globos, appellaverunt, scriptura vero divina coelos nominat : in quibus singulis primo quidem perspiciet ea, quae ibi geruntur, secundo vero etiam rationem quare gerantur agnoscet : et ita per ordinem digredietur singula, sequens eum, qui transgressus est coelos, Iesum filium Dei, dicentem : " Volo, ut ubi sum ego, et isti sint mecum." '

We shall now cite the evidence of Christian Apocalyptic works as attesting the prevalence of this belief in the seven heavens.

In the Apocalypse of Moses, p. 19 (*Apocalypses Apocryphae*, ed. Tischendorf, 1866), Eve is bidden to look up to the seven firmaments : ἀνάβλεψον τοῖς ὀφθαλμοῖς σου καὶ ἴδε τὰ ἑπτὰ στερεώματα ἀνεῳγμένα. On p. 21 Michael is bidden : ἄπελθε εἰς τὸν παράδεισον ἐν τῷ τρίτῳ οὐρανῷ. Thus the writer of this Apocalypse, so far as he touches on the subject of the seven heavens, agrees with the teaching of the Slavonic Enoch. In the Apoc. Esdrae (pp. 29, 30 *op. cit.*) there is mention made of a plurality of the heavens, and of Paradise as lying in the east. In the Apoc. Johannis (p. 84 *op. cit.*) the seven regions of the heavens are spoken of : καὶ γενήσεται κρότος μέγας ἐν τοῖς οὐρανοῖς, καὶ σαλευθήσονται τὰ ἑπτὰ (*a. l.* ἐννέα) πέταλα τοῦ οὐρανοῦ.

In our account of the third heaven according to the Slavonic Enoch, we showed that hell was situated in the north of that heaven. Similarly in the Testament of Isaac (*Testament of Abraham*, ed. James, pp. 146–8) hell is understood to be in one of the heavens. The same holds true of the Testament of Jacob (*op. cit.* p. 153), and of the Apoc. Esdrae, p. 29.

Finally in the Acts of Callistratus (ed. Conybeare), pp. 311–12, the seven circles of the heavens are mentioned.

Speculations about the seven heavens prevailed largely among the heretics. Thus according to Irenaeus, *contra Haer.* i. 5, 2, the Valentinians taught : ἑπτὰ γὰρ οὐρανοὺς κατεσκευακέναι, ὧν ἐπάνω τὸν δημιουργὸν εἶναι λέγουσι. Καὶ διὰ τοῦτο Ἑβδομάδα καλοῦσιν αὐτόν, τὴν δὲ μητέρα τὴν Ἀχαμὼθ Ὀγδοάδα . . . τοὺς δὲ ἑπτὰ οὐρανοὺς οὐκ (?) εἶναι νοητούς φασιν, ἀγγέλους δὲ αὐτοὺς ὑποτίθενται . . . ὡς καὶ τὸν παράδεισον ὑπὲρ τρίτον οὐρανὸν ὄντα, τέταρτον ἄγγελον λέγουσι δυνάμει ὑπάρχειν.

In Tertullian, *Adv. Valent.* xx, practically the same account is given : ' Tum ipsam caelorum septemplicem scenam solio desuper suo finit. Unde et Sabbatum dictus ab hebdomade sedis suae ... Caelos autem noeros deputant, et interdum angelos eos faciunt . . . sicut et Paradisum Archangelum quartum, quoniam et hunc supra caelum tertium pangunt.'

The heretic Marcus taught according to Hippolytus a similar doctrine of the heavens, but according to Irenaeus, *adv. Haer.* i. 17, 1, he reckoned eight heavens in addition to the sun and moon.

Basilides' view as to their being 365 heavens is well known (Augustine, *de Haer.* i. 4).

The Ophites (Irenaeus, *adv. Haer.* i. 30. 4, 5) believed in seven heavens ruled over by seven potentates, named Jaldabaoth, Jao, Sabaoth, Adoneus, Eloeus, Horeus, Asta-phaeus—a Hebdomad which with their mother Sophia formed a Ogdoad. A fuller account of this Hebdomad will be found in Origen, *contra Celsum*, vi. 31, and in Epiphanius *Haer.* xxvi. 10.

In the mysteries of Mithras described by Origen, *contra Celsum*, vi. 22, there are certain speculations akin to the doctrine of the seven heavens.

A fragment of Theodotus preserved by Clement is found regarding the creation of man : ὅθεν ἐν τῷ παραδείσῳ τῷ τετάρτῳ οὐρανῷ δημιουργεῖται [1].

The doctrine of the seven heavens, therefore, being associated with so many grotesque and incongruous features even in the thoughts of the orthodox, became in due time an offensive conception to the sounder minds in the Church, and this offensiveness was naturally aggravated by the important role it played in heretical theology. Augustine, though he expounds a peculiar doctrine of his own which asserts the existence of three heavens (*de Gen. ad Litt.* xii. 67), feels himself beset with abundant difficulties on this question. On the subject in general he writes : ' Si autem sic accipimus tertium coelum quo Apostolus raptus est, ut quartum etiam, et aliquot ultra

---

[1] The Valentinians also placed Paradise in the fourth heaven.

superius coelos esse credamus, infra quos et hoc tertium coelum, sicut eos alii septem, alii octo, alii novem vel decem perhibent . . . de quorum ratione sive opinione nunc disserere longum est' (*de Gen. ad Litt.* xii. 57). In the fourth century of the Christian era, Churchmen were required according to the clear tenor of Scripture to believe in the plurality of the heavens, but as to the number of these heavens they were at liberty to decide for themselves without prejudicing their orthodoxy. Thus Philastrius, Bishop of Brescia, at the close of the fourth century holds it a heresy to doubt the plurality of the heavens, but a man may without offence believe in seven, three, or two. ' De caelorum diversitate est haeresis quae ambigat. Scriptura enim in primo die caelum et terram facta declarat duo haec elementa, secundo firmamentum aquae factum, et nihilominus ipsum firmamentum caelum appellatum fuisse testatur. David autem dicit de caelis ita : *Laudate dominum caeli caelorum et aquae quae super caelos sunt.* Sive ergo sex caelos, secundum David, et septimum hoc firmamentum accipere quis voluerit, non errat; nam Solomon tres caelos dicit, ita : *Caelum et caelum caeli.* Paulus aeque apostolus usque ad tertium caelum se raptum fatetur. Sive ergo septem quis acceperit, ut David, sive tres, sive duos, non errat, quia et Dominus ait: *Pater qui in caelis est.*' (*De Haeres. Liber* xciv.)

But these and the like speculations had become so objectionable to the master mind of Chrysostom, that despite 2 Cor. xii. 2, 3 he declares the doctrine of a plurality of the heavens to be a mere device of man and contrary to holy scripture : τίς ἂν οὖν λοιπὸν μετὰ τὴν τοσαύτην διδασκαλίαν ἀνέχοιτο τῶν ἁπλῶς ἐξ οἰκείας διανοίας φθέγγεσθαι βουλομένων, καὶ ἀπεναντίως τῇ θείᾳ γραφῇ πολλοῖς οὐρανοῖς λέγειν ἐπιχειρούντων (*Hom. in Gen.* iv. 3). And again, in order to discredit the last traces of this view he maintains that the heaven neither revolves nor is spherical (*In Epist. ad Hebraeos, Hom.* xiv. 1).

Our task is now nearly done. It only remains for us to

point out that this doctrine, on its rejection by the Christian
Church, passed over with many similar ones into Mohammedanism. In fact, Mohammedanism formed in many respects
the *cloaca maxima* into which much of the refuse of Christianity
discharged itself.

Thus in the Koran xxiii it is written: 'And we have
created over you seven heavens, and we are not negligent of
what we have created.' And again in xli: 'And he formed
them into seven heavens in two days, and revealed unto every
heaven its office.'

Into a detailed representation of these heavens by later
Mohammedan writers it is not necessary for us to enter.

So far as I am aware every detail is borrowed from Jewish
and Christian Apocalypses. Some form of the Slavonic
Enoch seems to have been in Mohammed's hands[1].

[1] The four streams of Paradise
(Slav. En. viii. 5) which pour honey
and milk and oil and wine, reappear
in the Koran xlvii. Again, irrational
animals are to be restored to life at
the resurrection, to receive the recompense due to them, and then to return to the dust, with the exception
of Ezra's ass and the dog of the
seven sleepers (cf. Koran iii; xviii;
Sale's note on vi; Slav. Enoch lviii.
4-6).

THE

BOOK OF THE SECRETS OF ENOCH

THE SON OF ARED; A MAN WISE AND
BELOVED OF GOD [1].

—◆—

[*Concerning the Life and the Dream of Enoch [2].]

THERE was a very [3] wise man and a worker of great things :
God loved him, and received him, so that he should see the
heavenly abodes, the kingdoms of the wise, great, incon-
ceivable and never-changing God, the Lord of all, the
wonderful and glorious, and bright and all-beholding station
of the servants of the Lord, and the unapproachable throne
of the Lord, and the degrees and manifestations of the incorporeal hosts, and should be an eye-witness of the unspeakable ministrations. of the multitude of creatures, and of the
varying appearance, and indescribable singing of the host of
Cherubim, and of the immeasurable world.

I. 1. At that time he said: 'Hardly had I accomplished
*165 years, when I begat my son Methusal : after that I lived
200 years and accomplished all the years of my life [4], 365

---

[1] This general title appears in B as **These are the secret books of God
which were shown to Enoch.**
Introduction. THIS IS ENTIRELY WANTING IN B.   [2] Sok. om. I have
retained the headings of the Sections which are given in A, as they are
valuable for critical purposes; but as they do not belong to the original text
I have enclosed them in brackets.   [3] Sok. om.
I. [4] B om. ; Sok. supports text.

years.   2. *On the first day of the first month[1] I was alone in my house, *and I rested on my bed and slept.   3. And as I slept a great grief came upon my heart, and I wept with mine eyes[2] *in my dream, and I could not understand what this grief meant, or what would happen to me[3].   4. And there appeared to me two men very tall, such as I have never seen on earth.   5. And their faces *shone like the sun[4], and their eyes *were like burning lamps[5]; and fire came forth from their lips. *Their dress had the appearance of feathers: their feet were purple[6], *their wings were brighter than gold[7]; *their hands whiter than snow[3]. They stood at the head of my bed and called me by my name.   6. I awoke from my sleep and *saw clearly these men standing in front of me[8]. 7. I *hastened and[9] made obeisance to them and *was terrified, and the appearance of my countenance was changed[10] from fear.   8. And these[11] men said to me: "Be of good cheer, Enoch, be not afraid; the everlasting[12] God hath sent us to thee, and lo! to-day thou shalt ascend with us into heaven.

---

[1] In the second month on an appointed day, B; Sok. is conflate. [2] I had made myself melancholy weeping with my eyes, and I lay down on my bed to sleep, B.   [3] B om.; Sok. supports text.   [4] Were like the shining sun, Sok.   [5] Burnt like lamps, A.   [6] So Sok. A reads there was a conspicuousness in their raiment and singing, in appearance purple; B, their dress and singing were wonderful.   [7] And on their shoulders as it were golden wings, B.   [8] So Sok.; standing up quickly (?), B; A om.   [9] A B om.   [10] Veiled my face, B.   [11] The two, Sok.   [12] Almighty, B.

I. With verses 2, 3, cf. Eth. En. lxxxiii. 3, 5.   5. Faces shone like the sun: cf. xix. 1; Rev. i. 16; 4 Ezra [vi. 71]. Eyes were like burning lamps, from Dan. x. 6 עֵינָיו כְּלַפִּידֵי אֵשׁ: cf. Ezek. i. 13; Rev. i. 14; xix. 12. Fire came forth from their lips: cf. for language Rev. ix. 17; xi. 5. Their dress ... purple: the text is corrupt. Their hands whiter than snow; cf. Eth. En. cvi. 2, 10 'his body was whiter than snow': Apoc. Petri τὰ μὲν γὰρ σώματα αὐτῶν ἦν λευκότερα πάσης χιόνος.   7. Countenance was changed: Dan. v. 6, 9, 10.   8. Be of good cheer: Matt. ix. 2 θάρσει; xiv. 27; Mark vi. 50; x. 29; Acts xxiii. 11; xxvii. 22, 25. In LXX Gen. xxxv. 17; Exod. xiv. 13, &c. θάρσει is a rendering of אַל־תִּירָא Be not afraid: cf. 2 Kings i. 15; Ezek. ii. 6, &c.; Eth. En. xv. 1. The conjunction of Be of good cheer and

9. And tell thy sons and thy servants, all [1] *who work [2] *in thy house [3], and let no one seek thee, till the Lord bring thee back to them."   10. And I *hastened to obey [4] them, and went out *of my house [5]. And I called my sons Methusal, Regim [*and Gaidal [6]], and told them what wonderful [7] things *the two men [8] had said to me.'

[*The Instruction: how Enoch taught his Sons.*]

II. 1. 'Hear me, my children, for I do not know whither I am going, or what awaits me.   2. Now, my children, I say unto you: turn not aside from God: *walk before the face of the Lord and keep his judgements [9] *and do not worship vain gods [10], who did not make heaven and earth[11], for these

---

[1] That they are to do without thee on the earth A.   [2] A and Sok. om.   [3] Sok. om.   [4] Obeyed, B.   [5] B omits; A adds and shut the doors as was ordered me.   [6] B om.; Sok. supports text. See exegetical note *in loc.*   [7] B om.   [8] They, A; these men, Sok.

II. A om.   [9] Sok. adds do not defile the prayers offered for) your salvation, that the Lord may not shorten the work of your hands, and ye may not be deprived of the gifts of the Lord, and the Lord may not deprive you of the attainment of His gifts in your treasuries. Bless the Lord with the firstlings of your flocks and the firstlings of your children, and blessings shall be upon you for ever; and do not depart from the Lord.   [10] To vain creatures, A.   [11] Sok. adds nor any other creature.

Be not afraid is found in Matt. xiv. 27.   10. Sons: these are mentioned though not named in Eth. En. lxxxi. 5, 6; xci. 1. **Regim**: see lvii. 2. **Gaidal**: this name is derived from LXX Gen. iv. 18 ἐγεννήθη δὲ τῷ ʼΕνὼχ Γαϊδάδ. For Γαϊδάδ Mass. gives Irad (עִירָד) and Syriac Idar (ܝܕܪ), which more nearly approaches LXX. Observe that this Gaidal is the son of Enoch who is the *grandson of Cain*, and therefore wrongly appears here. As however B omits it both here and in lvii. 2, it is probably spurious. A confusion of Enoch, son of Lamech, and Enos, son of Seth, is to be found in the Clementine Recognitions iv. 12.

II. 1. **Know** whither I am going, &c.: cf. vii. 5.   2. **Turn not aside from** God: 1 Sam. xii. 20. **Walk before the face of the Lord**: Ps. lvi. 13; cxvi. 9. **Keep his judgements**: Lev. xviii. 5; Ezek. xxxvi. 27. **Worship vain gods**: Deut. viii. 19; cf. 1 Sam. (LXX, Syr., Vulg.) xii. 21. **Vain gods who did not make heaven and earth, for these will perish**, from Jer. x. 11; cf. Ps. xcvi. 5; Is. ii. 18; Acts xiv. 15 'Ye should turn from these vain things unto the living God, who made the heaven and the earth.' Jub. xii. 2, 3, 4 'What help . . . have we from those idols which thou dost worship . . . worship them not. Worship the God of heaven.'

will perish, * and also those who worship them [1].   3. * But may God make confident your hearts in the fear of Him [2]. 4. And now, my children, let no one seek me till the Lord brings me back to you.'

[*Of the taking up of Enoch; how the Angels took him up into the first heaven.*]

III. 1. It came to pass when I [3] had spoken to my sons, * these men [4] * summoned me and [5] took me on their wings [6] and placed me * on the clouds [7]. * And lo! the clouds moved [8]. 2. * And again (going) higher I saw the air and (going still) higher I saw the ether [9], and they placed me in the first heaven.   3. * And they showed me a very great sea, greater than the earthly sea [10].

[*Of the Angels who rule the Stars.*]

IV. 1. And they brought * before my face the elders, and the rulers of the orders of the stars [11], and they showed me the

---

[1] B om.   [2] But keep your hearts in the fear of God, B.   For the fear of Him A reads His own paths.
III. Instead of 'Of the taking up of Enoch, &c.' B reads ' The entry of Enoch into the first heaven.'   [3] Throughout this verse A speaks of Enoch in the third person.   [4] The angels, A.   [5] A om.   [6] A B add and brought me (him A) to the first heaven, which should be read at end of verse 2.   [7] There B.   [8] A B om.   [9] And there I gazed, and as I gazed higher I saw the air, A.   [10] B trans. after the 200 angels, iv. 1.
IV. [11] Me before the face of the elder, the ruler of the orders of the stars; and showed me their goings and comings from year to year, B.

---

3. Make confident your hearts in the fear of Him: Prov. xiv. 26.

III. 1. Placed me on the clouds. And lo! the clouds moved: cf. Eth. En. xiv. 8 ' the clouds invited me . . . and the winds gave me wings and drove me.'   The air . . . and the ether.   This corresponds to the firmament in Asc. Is. vii. 9 'Ascendimus in firmamentum et ibi vidi Sammaelem ejusque potestates . . . 13. et postea me ascendere fecit supra firma-mentum: hoc jam est (primum) coelum.'   3. A very great sea: cf. Rev. iv. 6; xv. 2 'sea of glass.'   In Test. xii. Patriarch. Levi 2 this sea lies between the first and second heavens, ὕδωρ κρεμάμενον ἀνάμεσον τούτου κἀκείνου.

IV. 1. Rulers of the orders of the stars, &c.   For a full but divergent account of these see Eth. En. lxxxii. 9-18, 20.   The 200 angels.   In the Eth. En. Uriel is the sole ruler of the

two hundred angels * who rule the stars and their heavenly
service ¹;   2. * And they fly with their wings ² * and go
round all (the stars) as they float ¹.

[*How the Angels guard the Habitations of the Snow.*]

V. 1. And * then I looked and saw ³ the treasuries of
the snow * and ice ⁴ and the angels ⁵ who guard their terrible ⁶
store-places;   2. And the treasuries of the clouds from
which they come forth and into which they enter.

[*Concerning the Dew and, the Oil, and different Colours.*]

VI. And they showed me the treasuries of the dew, like
* oil for anointing ⁷, * and its form was in appearance like
that of ⁸ all earthly colours ⁹ : also many ¹⁰ angels keeping their
treasuries, * and they shut and open them ¹⁰.

[*How Enoch was taken into the second Heaven¹¹.*]

VII. 1. And the men took me and brought me to the

---

¹ B om.   ² B reads immediately after earthly sea, iii. 3. Sok. om.
V. ³ They showed me, B. There I saw, Sok.   ⁴ A om.   ⁵ Terrible
angels, B.   ⁶ B om.
VI. ⁷ The balm of the olive tree, Sok.   ⁸ And the appearance of it
as also of, A. And their robes are like, B.   ⁹ May be rendered *flowers.*
¹⁰ B om.
VII. ¹¹ The Entry of Enoch into the second Heaven, B; Sok. om.

---

stars: cf. lxxii. 1; lxxx. 1. In Eth.
En. vi. 5 this is the number of angels
that apostatized.

V. 1. **Treasuries of the snow and
ice:** Job xxxviii. 22; cf. Eth. En.
lx. 17, 18. These treasuries are
placed in the second heaven by the
Test. xii. Patriarch. Levi 3 ὁ δεύτερος
(οὐρανὸς) ἔχει πῦρ χιόνα κρύσταλλον.
2. **Treasuries of the clouds:** cf.
Eth. En. lx. 19.

VI. 1. **Treasuries of the dew:**
cf. Eth. En. lx. 20. In the *Beresch.
rabba* c. 6, *Bammid'ar rabba*, c. 17,
and the *Chagiga* 12ᵇ, there is an

enumeration of the seven heavens.
The lowest of these which is called
וילן (Lat. velum) is empty. According to some, it appears in the morning
and disappears in the evening (see
Weber, p. 197): according to Bera-
choth 58ᵇ the Wilôn is rolled up in
order that the light of the second
heaven, the Rakia, may be seen.
This heaven seems also to be empty
according to the Test. xii. Patr. Levi
3 ὁ κατώτερος διὰ τοῦτο στυγνότερός
ἐστιν ἐπειδὴ οὗτος ὁρᾷ πάσας ἀδικίας
ἀνθρώπων.

second heaven, and showed me [1] *the darkness, and there I saw [2] the prisoners suspended [3], reserved for (and) awaiting [3] the eternal [4] judgement.   2. * And these angels were gloomy in appearance, more than the darkness of the earth [3].   *And they unceasingly wept every hour [5], and I said to the men who were with me: 'Why are these men continually [3] tortured?'   3. *And the men [6] answered me: 'These are they who apostatized from *the Lord [7]: who obeyed not the commandments of God, and took counsel of their own will *and transgressed together with their prince and have been already confined to the second heaven [8].   4. And I felt great pity for them.   *And lo! the angels [9] made obeisance to me, and said to me: "O man of God! *pray for us to the Lord [10]."   5. And I answered [11] them: "Who am I, a mortal

---

[1] Sok. adds and I saw. [2] B om.; after darkness, A adds greater than the darkness on earth. [3] B om. [4] Great and immeasurable, A; immeasurable, Sok. [5] And I saw those who were condemned weeping, B. [6] And they, A; The men, Sok. [7] God, A. [8] B om. For second A Sok. read fifth. [9] They, A; and these angels, Sok. [10] Oh! that thou wouldst pray to God for us! B. [11] Sok. adds and said unto.

VII. 1. The darkness and... the prisoners... reserved for... judgement: cf. 2 Pet. ii. 4 'Committed them (the angels that sinned as here) to pits of darkness to be reserved unto judgement.' These prisoners are the angels that 'kept not their first estate' and are 'reserved... under darkness unto the judgement of the great day,' Jude 6. They appear to be referred to also in Test. xii. Patr. Levi 3 ἐν αὐτῷ (τῷ δευτέρῳ οὐρανῷ) εἰσὶ πάντα τὰ πνεύματα τῶν ἐπαγωγῶν εἰς ἐκδίκησιν τῶν ἀνόμων, where ἐπαγωγῶν seems corrupt. Observe that the angels who sinned with women are imprisoned *under the earth* in the Eth. En. x as also in our text xviii. 7. On the other hand the angels who sinned through lust

for empire are prisoners in the second heaven. 3. Took counsel of their own will. For phraseology cf. Eph. i. 11; Is. xlvi. 10. These angels wished to form a kingdom of their own. Cf. Weber, p. 244. Their prince Satanail: xviii. 3. Second heaven. This emendation is necessary. When the angels of the fifth heaven rebelled they were cast down to the second heaven and imprisoned there. 4. The angels ask Enoch to intercede for them, exactly as in Eth. En. xiii. 4. 'They besought me to draw up a petition that they might find forgiveness.' Man of God: Deut. xxxiii. 1; 1 Tim. vi. 11; 2 Tim. iii. 17. 5. Cf. Eth. En. xv. 2 'Say to the watchers of heaven... you should intercede for men and not men

man, that I should pray for angels? Who knows whither I go,
or what awaits me: or who prays * for me [1]?".'

[* *Of the taking of Enoch to the third Heaven* [2].]

VIII. 1. And these men took me from thence, and brought
me to the third heaven, and placed me * in the midst of
a garden [3]—* a place [4] such as has never been known for * the
goodliness of its appearance [5].   2. And * I saw [6] all the
trees of beautiful colours and [7] their fruits ripe * and fragrant [6],
and all kinds of * food which they produced [8], springing up with
delightful fragrance [9].   3. And in the midst (there is) the
tree of life, in that place, on which God rests, when He comes
into Paradise. And this tree cannot be described for its
* excellence and sweet odour [10].   4. And it is beautiful
more than any created thing. And on all sides in appearance
it is like gold and crimson and transparent as fire, and
it covers everything [11].   5. * From its root in the

---

[1] B om.

VIII. [2] Entry into the third Heaven, B.   [3] So B and Sok. A reads There,
I looked below and I saw gardens.   [4] I looked below and saw that place,
Sok.   [5] Their goodliness, A and Sok.   [6] B om.   [7] And I beheld, A.   [8] Agree-
able food, B.   [9] B adds and four rivers flowing with soft course and every
kind of thing good that grows for food. These words belong to verse 6.   [10] The
excellence of its sweet odour, B.   [11] The whole garden, Sok. After this
A adds and the gardens have all kinds of fruits; Sok. adds and the garden
has all kinds of trees planted and all fruits. B OMITS VERSE 4.

---

for you. Who knows whither I go,
&c.: cf. ii. 1.

VIII. 1. A garden: as in 2 Cor. xii.
2, 4 Paradise is placed in the third
heaven.   2. All the trees . . . fragrant : cf. Gen. ii. 9 ; Eth. En. xxix. 2 ;
Apoc. Mosis (p. 20) . . . All kinds
of food which they produced: cf.
Rev. xxii. 2 'Bearing twelve manner
of fruits.'   3. In the midst the
tree of life: Gen. ii. 9. This is a
familiar feature in Jewish Apocalypses. Cp. Eth. En. xxv. 4, 5 ; Rev.
ii. 7 ; xxii. 2, 14 ; 4 Ezra vii. 53 ; viii.
52 ; Test. Levi 18. See also Iren.
i. 5, 2. When we come to Epiphanius

we find it denounced as a Mani-
chaean doctrine, *Haer.* 66, p. 278.
The tree of life . . . on which
God rests. This is reproduced in
a modified form in the Apoc. Pauli
(ed. Tischend. p. 64) δένδρον παμμεγέθη
ὡραῖον, ἐν ᾧ ἐπανεπαύετο τὸ πνεῦμα
ἅγιον. There is a modification of this
idea in Apoc. Mosis (ed. Tischend.
p. 12) καὶ ὁ θρόνος τοῦ θεοῦ ὅπου ἦν τὸ
ξύλον τῆς ζωῆς ἐντρεπίζετο.   5. From
its root, &c. This is the source of
the words in Apoc. Pauli (ed. Tischend.
p. 64) καὶ ἐκ τῆς ῥίζης ·αὐτοῦ ἐξήρχετο πᾶν εὐωδέστατον ὕδωρ, μεριζόμενον εἰς τέσσαρα ὀρύγματα. The

garden[1] there go forth four[2] streams which pour honey and milk[3], oil and wine, and are separated in four directions, and go about with a soft course.   6. And they go down to the Paradise of Eden, between corruptibility and incorruptibility. And thence[4] they go along the earth, and have a revolution in their circle like also the other elements[5].   7. * And there is another tree, an olive tree always distilling oil[6]. And there is no tree there without fruit, and every tree[7] is blessed[8]. 8. And there are * three hundred angels very glorious, who keep the garden[9], and with never ceasing voices and blessed singing, they serve the Lord * every day[10]. And I said[11]: 'What a very[12] blessed place is this!' And those men spake unto me:

[*The showing to Enoch of the Righteous, and the Place of Prayers.*]

IX. 'This place, O Enoch, is prepared for the righteous

---

[1] Emended with Apoc. Pauli from its root; B omits; A and Sok. add in the going out towards earth Paradise is between corruptibility and incorruptibility. This is clearly a corrupt addition. See quotation from Apoc. Pauli in explanatory notes.   [2] Two, A and Sok.   See note 9 on p. 7 for text of B.   [3] A adds and the streams pour.   [4] Sok. adds they go forth and are divided into forty (four ?) and; B omits verse 6.   [5] Sok. adds of the air.   [6] A Sok. om.   [7] Place, A.   [8] Sok. adds in its fruit and every place is blessed.   [9] Angels guarding them, very bright in appearance, B.   [10] Every day and hour, A; the whole day, Sok.   [11] A adds lo!   [12] B om.

---

writer has tried to reduce to one organic conception the two originally different conceptions of the heavenly and the earthly Paradise. The latter seems to have been the older: Gen. ii. 8–17; Eth. En. xxxii. 3–6; lxxvii. 3. The heavenly Paradise is referred to in Eth. En. lx. 8; lxi. 12; lxx. 3. Four streams which pour honey and milk and oil and wine. Cf. Apoc. Pauli (ed. Tischend. p. 52) ποταμοὶ τέσσαρες ἐκύκλουν αὐτήν, ῥέοντες μέλι καὶ γάλα καὶ ἔλαιον καὶ οἶνον. These four streams are taken over into the Koran xlvii, save that

instead of a river of oil there is a river of incorruptible water. The earthly Paradise is said to be between corruptibility and incorruptibility, because existence in it was a probation and might issue either in corruptibility or incorruptibility: or because it lay on the confines of the regions of corruptibility and incorruptibility.   7. Another tree ... distilling oil: Cf. xxi. 7. These are the *arbor misericordiae* and the *oleum misericordiae* of Evang. Nicodemi ii. 3: cf. ch. xxii. 8.

IX. 1. Prepared for the righteous:

who endure * every kind of attack [1] * in their lives [2] * from those who [3] afflict their souls : who turn away their eyes from unrighteousness, and accomplish a righteous judgement, and also give bread to the hungry, and clothe the naked, and raise the fallen, and assist the * orphans who are [4] oppressed, and who walk * without blame [4] before the face of the Lord, and serve him only. For them this place is prepared as an eternal inheritance.'

[*Here they showed Enoch the terrible Places, and various Tortures.*]

X. 1. And the men then [5] led me to the Northern region [6], and showed me there [7] a very terrible place.   2. And there are all sorts of tortures in that place. Savage [7] darkness and impenetrable [7] gloom ; and there is no light there [7], * but

---

IX. [1] Attacks, B.   [2] A om.   [3] Who, B.   [4] B om.
X. [5] Removed me from thence and, B.   [6] Part of the heavens, B.
[7] B om.

---

cf. Matt. xxv. 34. See note on Eth. En. lx. 8. **Turn away their eyes from unrighteousness** : Ps. cxix. 37 ; cf. Is. xxxiii. 15. **Execute righteous judgement** : Ezek. xviii. 8. **Give bread to the hungry, and clothe the naked** : Ezek. xviii. 7 : cf. Tob. iv. 16 ; 4 Ezra ii. 20 ; Or. Sibyll. ii. 83 ; viii. 404-405. **Assist the orphans who are oppressed** : cf. Is. i. 17 ; Jer. xxii. 3, 16. **Walk without blame before . . . the Lord** : cf. Luke i. 6. **Eternal inheritance** : cf. Heb. ix. 15.

X. 1. **Northern region.** To the modern mind it may seem strange that a division of heaven should be assigned to the wicked, but this idea presented no difficulty to the Jews and early Christians. Thus in the O. T. Satan can present himself in heaven, Job i. 7, 8 ; while in the N. T. evil may not only appear, but can also have a settled habitation there : Eph. vi. 12 ' the spiritual hosts of wickedness in the heavens ' (ἐν τοῖς ἐπουρανίοις). In Rev. xii. 7, 8, 9 this condition of things is represented as being at an end. Satan is cast out of heaven with his angels, and the sphere of his activity and residence is now limited to the earth, Rev. xii. 12. The old idea of wickedness being in heaven reappears in Test. Levi 3, where however it is limited to the second heaven (see also Test. Isaac 146, 147 ; Test. Jacob 153) ; but it was subsequently banished from Christian and Jewish thought. See Introduction. 2. **Darkness and . . . gloom** : Apoc. Petri 12 τόπῳ σκοτεινῷ : Apoc. Pauli, p. 62, where one region of a gloomy fire is always burning [1], * and a fiery river goes forth [2]. * And all that place has fire on all sides, and on all sides [3] cold and ice, * thus it burns and freezes [4].　3. * And the prisoners are very savage [2]. And the angels terrible and without pity, carrying savage [2] weapons, and their torture was unmerciful. 4. And I said : * 'Woe, woe [2]! How terrible is this place [5]!' And the men said to me : 'This place,

---

[1] Neither fire nor flame and a gloom is over that place, B.　[2] B. om.
[3] In that place; on both sides fire and on both sides, Sok.; B om.　[4] So Sok. A reads thirst and freezing, B; and murkiness.　[5] What a terrible place is this! A.

Hades is said σκότους καὶ ζόφους πεπληρωμένον. There is no light there : quoted by Apoc. Pauli (p. 57) οὐκ ἦν ἐκεῖ φῶς. Fiery river. This idea appears first in Eth. En. xiv. 19 ; Dan. vii. 10, but not there as an instrument of punishment. It seems however to have been applied early to that purpose, as here, and in the form of a lake of fire in Rev. xix. 20 ; xx. 10, 14, 15 ; xxi. 8. Or. Sibyll. ii. 196-200, 252-253, 286 ; iii. 84 ; viii. 411 : cf. Apoc. Petri 8 λίμνη τις ἦν μεγάλη πεπληρωμένη βορβόρου φλεγομένου. Apoc. Pauli (ed. Tischend. p. 57) ἔνθα ἐπέρρεεν ποταμὸς πύρινος. In Clem. Alex. *Exc. Theod.* 38 the two ideas are combined : ποταμὸς ἐκπορεύεται πυρὸς ὑποκάτω τοῦ θρόνου τοῦ τόπου, καὶ ῥεῖ εἰς τὸ κενὸν τοῦ ἐκτισμένου, ὅ ἐστιν ἡ γέεννα (quoted by James, *Test. Abraham*, p. 160). Fire on all sides, and on all sides cold and ice. This seems to be drawn from Eth. En. xiv. 13, where God's dwelling in heaven is said to be 'hot as fire and cold as ice.' 3. Angels terrible and without pity, carrying savage weapons. Angels of destruction are

mentioned in the O. T. 2 Sam. xxiv. 16 ; 2 Kings xix. 35 ; I Chron. xxi. 15. A class of destroying angels may be referred to in Ecclus. xxxix. 28 πνεύματα, ἃ εἰς ἐκδίκησιν ἔκτισται. In Eth. En. liii. 3, 4 ; lvi. 1 ; lxii. 11 ; lxiii. 1, a class of evil angels whose sole function is to punish is mentioned and the conception is evidently a familiar one, though here found for the first time in Jewish literature. This idea appears in the N. T. Rev. ix. 11, 15 ; xvi. Of these the angel mentioned in ix. 11 is Ἀπολλύων. In Matt. xiii. 49 good angels cast the wicked into the furnace of fire. These angels of destruction or punishment are frequently referred to in Latin literature. Test. Levi 3 αἱ δυνάμεις... οἱ ταχθέντες εἰς ἡμέραν κρίσεως, ποιῆσαι ἐκδίκησιν ἐν τοῖς πνεύμασι τῆς πλάνης. These angels of punishment are placed in the third heaven as in our text. Cf. Apoc. Petri 6 οἱ κολάζοντες ἄγγελοι : 8 ἄγγελοι βασανισταί. The words angels terrible and without pity, carrying savage weapons seem to have been before the writer of Test. Abraham A. xii ἄγγελοι . . . ἀνηλεεῖς τῇ γνώμῃ καὶ ἀπότομοι τῷ

Enoch, is prepared for * those who do not honour God; who
commit evil deeds on earth, vitium sodomiticum, witchcraft [1],
enchantments, devilish [2] magic; and who boast of their evil [2]
deeds, * stealing, lying, calumnies, envy, evil thoughts, fornication, and murder [2].   5. Who steal [3] the souls of wretched [2]
men [4], oppressing [5] * the poor and spoiling them of their possessions [2], and themselves grow rich * by the taking of other men's
possessions [6], * injuring them [7].   Who when they might feed
the hungry, allow them to die of famine; who when they
might clothe them, strip them naked.   6. Who do not
know their Creator and have worshipped * gods without life;
who can neither see nor hear, being [2] vain gods, * and have
fashioned the forms of idols, and bow down to a contemptible
thing, made with hands [2]; for all these this place is prepared
for an eternal inheritance.

[* *Here they took Enoch to the fourth Heaven, where is the
Course of the Sun and Moon* [8].]

XI. i. And the men took me and conducted me to the
fourth heaven, and showed me all * the comings and [9] goings
forth and all the rays of the light of the sun and moon.

---

[1] The impure who have done godlessness on the earth, who practise,
B.   [2] B om.   [3] B adds secretly.   [4] B adds who bind them with
a galling yoke.   [5] Who see, A; B om.   [6] And in order to
acquire the goods of strangers, A.   [7] Oppress them, A; B om.
   XI. [8] Entry of Enoch into the fourth Heaven, B.   [9] A om.

βλέμματι ... ἀνηλέως τύπτοντες αὐτοὺς
ἐν πυρίναις χαρζαναῖς. 4. Prepared
for those who do not honour God.
Contrast Matt. xxv. 41. *Vitium sodo-
miticum.* Cf. Apoc. Petri 17 : Test.
Isaac (James' ed.), p. 148.   6. Cf.
Lev. xix. 4; xxvi. 1; Or. Sibyll.
v. 77–85; viii. 378–81; 395–98;
Fragm. i. 20–22; iii. 21–45.
   XI. 1. Fourth heaven. According

to the Rabbinic tradition *Chagiga* 12 [b]
the fourth heaven was called זבול
and it was said to contain the heavenly
Jerusalem, the temple, the altar, and
Michael who offered daily sacrifice.
The following quotation (ἐκ τῶν Θεο-
δότου ... 'Επιτομαί) seems to agree
with the Rabbinic view: ὅθεν ἐν τῷ
παραδείσῳ τῷ τετάρτῳ οὐρανῷ δημιουργεῖται. **Comings and goings** ...

* And I measured [1] their goings, * and computed their light.
2. And I saw that [2] the sun has a light * seven times [3] greater
than the moon.   * I beheld their circle, and their chariot [4] on
which * each goes [5] like a wind * advancing with astonishing
swiftness [6], and * they have [7] no rest day or night coming or
going.   3. There are four great stars ; * each star has
under it a thousand stars [6] at the right of the chariot of the
sun ; and four at the left [8], * each having under it a thousand
stars, altogether eight thousand [6].   4. * Fifteen myriads
of [9] angels go * out with the sun and attend him during the
day, and by night one thousand [6].   * Each angel has six
wings. They go [10] before the chariot of the sun [11].   5. And
a hundred angels * keep warm and light up the sun [12].

[*Of the wonderful Creatures of the Sun.*]

XII. 1. * And I looked and saw other flying creatures,
their names phoenixes and chalkadri wonderful and strange

---

[1] Their dimensions, B.   [2] And I saw their goings, B.   [3] A om.
[4] His circle and his chariot, A ; and around them is a chariot, B.   [5] They
go always, A.   [6] B om.   [7] He has, A.   [8] B adds always going
with the sun.   [9] Fifteen, A ; B om.   [10] Six winged creatures
go with the angels, A ; B om.   [11] A adds in a fiery flame.   [12] Minister
unto him fire, Sok. ; B om. verse 5.

---

of the sun and moon : cf. Eth. En.
lxxii–lxxviii. 2. The sun has a light
seven times, &c.: Eth. En. lxxii.
37. Their chariot on which each
goes like a wind : Eth. En. lxxii. 5
'the chariots on which he (the sun)
ascends are driven by the wind': so
also of the moon in Eth. En. lxxiii. 2
and of both in lxxv. 3 ; lxxxii. 8.
Have no rest day or night : Eth.
En. xli. 7 '(the sun and moon) rest
not' : lxxii. 37 'rests not . . . day
and night.' Sibyllines iii. 21 'Ηέλιόν
τ' ἀκάμαντα. 3, 4. There is nothing
corresponding to these verses in Eth.
En. 5. Cf. Eth. En. lxxv. 4.

XII. 1. Phoenixes and chalkadri. This seems to be the only
reference to such creatures in literature. The phoenix, which according
to all ancient writers was solitary and
unique ('unus in terris,' Tac. *Ann.* vi.
28 ; cf. Mart. v. 7 ; Ovid, *Met.* xv.
392) in its kind, is here represented as
one of a class. The phoenix is mentioned in Job xxix. 18 according to
Jewish authorities, where for 'I shall
multiply my days as the sand' they
render 'as the phoenix' כחול. There
are many references to it among
the Greeks and Romans : Herod. ii.
73 ; Tac. *Ann.* vi. 28 ; Ovid, *Met.* xv.

in appearance, with the feet and tails of lions, and the heads
of crocodiles [1]; * their appearance was of a purple colour, like

---

XII. [1] And the flying creatures are in form like two birds, one like
a phoenix and the other like a chalkedry. And in their shape they
resemble a lion in their feet and tail and in the head a crocodile, Sok.;
B om.

392; Mart. *Epigr.* v. 7, 1; Stat.
Sylv. ii. 4, 37; Plin. *N. H.* x. 2. The
fable regarding it is recounted as sober
fact by 1 Clem. *ad Corinth.* xxv;
Tertullian, *de Resurrect. Carn.* xiii;
Ambrose, *Hexaem.* v. 23; Epiphanius,
Ancorat. lxxxiv; and the *Apostolic
Constitutions* v. 7. Origen, *contra
Celsum* iv. 98, doubts it: so also Greg.
Naz. *Orat.* xxxi, 10, and among the
later Greeks Maximus and Photius,
and among the Latins Augustine *de
Anima* iv. 33. To those who believed
the fable we should add Rufinus
Comment. in Symb. Apost. xi. and the
Pseudo-Lactantius, from whose poem
De Phoenice we draw the following
references, which seem to be derived
either directly or indirectly from our
text. The phoenix in that poem is an
attendant of the sun, 'satelles phoebi'
ver. 33, as in xii. 2 are the phoenixes:
when the sun appears it greets him
with strains of sacred song (verses
43-50) and claps its wings (verses
51-54) exactly as the phoenixes in
xv. 1. This poem belongs probably to the fourth century. The
voice of the phoenix was celebrated
for its sweetness: cf. the Jewish poet
Ezekiel v. 10 φωνὴν δὲ πάντων εἶχεν
εὐπρεπεστάτην: Pseudo-Lactantius,
de Phoenice 46 'miram vocem': 56
'innarrabilibus sonis.' Its colour
was purple—purpureus (Pliny); κυά-
νεός ἐστιν ῥόδοις ἐμφερής (Achil.
Tat.), cf. xv. 1 and xii. 1. On
the two different legends in the
Talmud about the origin of the
phoenix see Hamburger, *R. E.*

für Talmud 908-9. On the question generally see Lightfoot, and
Gebhardt and Harnack on 1 *Clem.*
xxv. 1; Eckermann in *Ersch und
Grueber* sect.iii.xxiv.310-16; Creuzer,
Symbol. und Mythol. ii. 163 (third
ed.); Piper, *Mythol. und Symbol. der
Christl. Kunst* i. 446, 471; Ebert,
*Allgemeine Geschichte der Litera-
tur des Mittelalters* i. 93-98; Seyf-
farth, *Z. D. M. G.* 1849, 63-89;
Gundert, *Z. f. luth. Theol.* 1854,
451-54. **Chalkadri.** This may be
a transliteration of Χαλκύδραι, brazen
hydras, or serpents. They are classed
with the Cherubim in Eth. En. xx. 7
'Gabriel . . . who is over Paradise
and the Serpents (τῶν δρακόντων in
the Greek) and the Cherubim.' Hence
they seem to have been a class of
heavenly creatures, i. e. the Seraphim
שְׂרָפִים. The idea of flying serpents
was a familiar one from the O. T. Is.
xiv. 29; xxx. 6 שָׂרָף מְעוֹפֵף. It was
not unfamiliar to the rest of the
ancient world: cf. Herod. ii. 75;
Lucan ix. 729-30; Ovid, *Met.* v.
642-4; *Fast.* iv. 562; also Claudian,
Valerius Flaccus, Ammianus,
Aelian, Apollonius. In the O. T.
these flying serpents are venomous in
such passages as Num. xxi. 6; Deut.
viii. 15; Is. xiv. 29; xxx. 6. What
relation these seraphim bear to those
in Is. vi. 2, 6 it is hard to determine.
That these latter were winged dragons
we must assume according to Delitzsch
(*Das Buch Jesaia*, pp. 124, 5). The
analogy of the animal-like forms of
the Cherubim in Ezek. i. 5-11 is

the rainbow; their size nine hundred measures [1].   2. *Their wings were like those of angels, each with twelve, and they attend the chariot of the sun, and go with him [2], bringing heat and dew *as they are ordered by God [3].   3. *So the sun makes his revolutions, and goes [4] *under the heavens,

---

[1] B om.   [2] So A and Sok., but that the former omits chariot of the. Twelve flying spirits and twelve wings to each angel who accompanies the chariot, B.   [3] And as he is ordered by God, Sok.   [4] B om.; A adds and proceeds.

---

certainly in favour of this view. The serpent was anciently a symbol of wisdom and healing among the Greeks, the Egyptians (Brugsch, *Rel. und Myth.* pp. 103, 4), and the Hebrews, Num. xxi. 8, 9 ; 2 Kings xviii. 4 : Matt. x. 16; John iii. 14. Hezekiah's destruction of the 'brazen serpent' as associated with idolatry may have caused the symbol to bear almost without exception an evil significance in later times, so that at last it became a designation of Satan : cf. Rev. xii. 9. We are therefore inclined to identify these Chalkadri with the Seraphim or heavenly creatures of Isaiah vi. These Chalkadri, we should add, sing in xv. 1 as do the Seraphim in Is. vi. 3, though their functions in the main are different. The idea here appears in a developed form and is no doubt indebted for its enlargement to Egyptian mythology. The Seraphim first appear in conjunction with other orders of angels in Eth. En. lxi. 10. Here their original character seems already to have been forgotten almost as wholly as in modern days, and they are regarded merely as a special class of angels ; whereas in *Eth. En.* xx. 7 their true nature is still borne in mind. In the N. T. neither Cherubim nor Seraphim appear, but the character-

istics of both reappear, fused together in the 'four living creatures' of Rev. iv. 6-8. However, though the N. T. takes no notice of the Seraphim save the indirect one of Rev. iv. 6-8, the conception obtained in later times the recognition of the Church through Dionysius the Areopagite's scheme of the nine heavenly orders. See Cheyne's *Prophecies of Isaiah,* i. 36, 42 ; ii. 283-6. **Feet and tails of lions.** The feet of the Cherubim in Ezek. i. 7 are like calves' feet. **Their size nine hundred measures.** In Bochart's *Hierozoicon* iii. 225-227 we find by citations from Strabo, Aelian, Valerius, Philostorgius, Diodorus, &c., that the ancients were ready to believe in monstrous dragons or serpents. Aelian, for instance, speaks of one 210 feet long, while an Arabian writer describes one of 8,000 paces in length. In the Talmud there is frequent mention of angels and creatures of a like monstrous size. **2. Each with twelve.** As the ordinary angels in xi. 4 have six wings each, these creatures are assigned twelve each. It would seem more natural to read this verse immediately after xi. 5 ; xii. 1 however must in some form and in some place appear in the text, as we see from xv. 1. **Bringing heat and dew.** Contrast

and goes under [1] the earth with the light * of his beams unceasingly [2].

[*The Angels took Enoch, and placed him on the East at the Gates of the Sun.*]

XIII. 1. These men brought me to the East [3] and * showed me the gates [4] by which the sun * goes forth [5] at the appointed seasons, and according to the revolution of the months * of the whole year [6], and * according to the number of the hours, day and night [7]. 2. And I saw the six great [8] gates * open, each gate having sixty-one stadia and a quarter of one stadium [6]; * and I truly measured them and understood their size to be so much [9], by which the sun goes forth; and he goes to the west * and makes his course correspond. And he proceeds through all the months [6]. 3. * And by the first gates he goes out forty-two days; by the second gates thirty-five days; by the fourth gates thirty-five; by the fifth gates thirty-five; by the sixth gates [8] forty-five [10]. 4. * And so he returns [11] * from the sixth gates in the course of time [6] : * and he enters by the fifth gates during thirty-five days, by the fourth gates thirty-five, by the third gates during thirty-five days; by the second gates thirty-five [10]. 5. * And so the

---

[1] To descend upon, B ; under the heaven and under, Sok. [2] The rays of the sun, B ; Of his beams, Sok.
XIII. [3] B adds of the heavens. [4] Placed me at the gates of the sun, A. [5] Enters, B. [6] B om. [7] At the shortening up to the lengthening of the days and nights, B. [8] A om. [9] And I measured their size, and I could not comprehend their size, B. [10] A B om. [11] B om. A adds to rest.

---

the conception in Æth. En. lx. 20. 3. Goes under the earth. This is undoubtedly corrupt, as the sun does not go under the earth but through the fourth heaven when he sets in the west. See xiv. 2 (note). Unceasingly : cf. xi. 2 (note).

XIII. 1. The gates by which the sun goes forth. These are the six gates mentioned in the next verse. For an account of the sun's six eastern gates and six western see Eth. En. lxxii. 2-4. Six gates: Eth. En. lxxii. 3. The rest of the chapter is hopelessly corrupt. The account seems to be derived originally from Eth. En.

days of the whole year[1] are finished according to the alternation of the four[2] seasons.

[*They took Enoch to the West.*]

XIV. 1. And *then these[3] men took me to the * West of the heavens[4] and showed me six great gates open, * corresponding to the Eastern gates[5], opposite * to which the sun goes out by the Eastern gates[6], according to the number of the days * three hundred and sixty-five, and the quarter of a day[7].   2. * So he sets by the Western gates[8].   When he goes out by the Western gates[9] * four hundred angels

---

[1] By his regular departure the years, B. And so the whole year, A.
[2] B om.
XIV. [3] The, B.   [4] Western regions, A.   [5] Corresponding to the Eastern entrance, B. Opposite to the circuit of the Eastern gates, Sok.
[6] Where the sun retires, A. By which the sun passes, Sok.   [7] B om.
[8] A om.   [9] A adds he conceals his light under the earth and the glories of his luminary.

---

lxxii. 2–37.   5. Four seasons: cf. xl. 6. The account of two of these seasons is found in Eth. En. lxxxii. 15–20: that of the remaining two is lost.

XIV. 1. Three hundred and sixty-five, and the quarter of a day. I have shown in my edition of the Eth. En. pp. 190–91 that the writer of chs. lxxii–lxxxii. was familiar with the solar year of 365¼ days, but that owing to national prejudices he refused to acknowledge it.   2. According to the Eth. En. lxxii. 5 the sun returns after sunset through the north in order to reach the east. In our text, however, the sun revolves through the fourth heaven, xi; xxx. 3, and when he rises in the east goes under the heavens and appears to men. During the night while he passes through

the fourth heaven he is *without light,* or in the words of the text *his crown is taken from him:* when he is about to reappear in the east his crown, or in other words his light, is restored to him. The reason why the sun is obliged to surrender his crown in passing through the fourth heaven before God is presumably that which is given in the Apoc. Mosis (ed. Tischend. p. 19): the sun cannot shine before the Light of the Universe (ἐνώπιον τοῦ φωτὸς τῶν ὅλων). The passage in this Apocalypse appears undoubtedly to be founded on the present text. Eve is there represented as seeing the sun and moon praying for Adam before God but *without their light.* She thereupon asks: ποῦ ἐστὶν τὸ φῶς αὐτῶν, καὶ διὰ τί γεγόνασιν μελανοειδεῖς; καὶ λέγει αὐτῇ Σήθ. οὐ δύνανται φαίνειν ἐνώπιον τοῦ φωτὸς

take his crown and bring it to the Lord[1].   3. And the sun
revolves[2] in his chariot * and goes without light[3] * for
seven complete hours in the night[4].   * And when he comes
near the East[5] * at the eighth hour of the night[6], * the four
hundred angels bring his crown and crown him[7].

[*The Creatures of the Sun; the Phoenixes and Chalkidri sang.*]

XV. 1. Then sang the creatures[8] called the Phoenixes and
the Chalkidri.   On this account every bird claps its wings,
rejoicing at the giver of light, * and they sang a song at the
command of the Lord[9].   2. The giver of light comes to
give his brightness to * the whole world[10].   3. * And they
showed me the calculation of the going of the sun.   And the
gates by which he enters and goes out are great gates, which
God made for the computation of the year[11].   4. * On this
account the sun is great[12].

---

[1] So B and Sok., but that the former reads four instead of four hundred.
A reads but the crown of his splendour is in heaven before the Lord:
and there are four hundred angels attending Him.   [2] Revolves,
B Sok.   Goes under the earth, A.   [3] And rests, A.   [4] B om.;
A Sok. support text, but that Sok. omits complete. After night A adds
and reaches half his course under the earth.   [5] At the Eastern
gates, B; Sok. om.   [6] B om.   [7] He brings forth his luminary
and his shining crown, and the sun is lighted up more than fire, A.
And places on it again the crown, B.
  XV.   [8] A adds of the sun; B OMITS VERSES 1, 2.   [9] Singing with their
voices, Sok.   [10] His creation, Sok.; A adds and there will be the
guards of the morning, which are the rays of the sun and the earthly
sun will go out and will receive his brightness to light up all the face
of the earth.   [11] So A and Sok. B reads this arrangement of the gates
by which he enters and goes out the two angels showed me; these
gates the Lord made for the computation and his yearly record of the
sun.   [12] B om.; A adds its revolutions extend to twenty-eight years,
and so it was from the beginning.

τῶν ὅλων, καὶ τούτου χάριν ἐκρύβη τὸ
φῶς ἀπ' αὐτῶν. 3. Seven complete
hours in the night. This is corrupt.
The writer must have known that the
length of the night varied with the season. In the Eth. En. a chapter (lxxii)
is devoted to the explanation of the
varying lengths of the day and night.

XV. 1. See xii. 1 (note). Every
bird. We should expect 'all these
winged creatures,' i. e. the Phoenixes
and Chalkidri. Or are we to take it
that the early song of birds at sun-
rise is here referred to? but this is
unlikely.

[*The Men took Enoch and placed him at the East, at the Course of the Moon.*]

XVI. 1. *The other, the computation of the moon these men showed me[1]; *all the goings and revolutions[2]. *And they pointed out the gates to me[3], twelve great[4] gates extending *from the West to the East[5], by which the moon enters *and goes out[6] at the customary times.   2. She enters *the first gate when the sun is in the West thirty-one days exactly[7]; by the second gate thirty-one[8] days exactly; by the third gate thirty days exactly; by the fourth gate thirty days exactly; by the fifth gate thirty-one days exactly; by the sixth gate thirty-one days exactly; by the seventh gate thirty days exactly; by the eighth gate thirty-one days exactly; by the ninth gate thirty-one[9] days exactly; by the tenth gate thirty[10] exactly; by the eleventh gate thirty-one days exactly; by the twelfth gate twenty-eight days[11] exactly.   3. And so by the Western gates in her revolutions, and corresponding to the number of the Eastern gates she goes, and accomplishes the year[12].   4. *And unto the sun there are three hundred and sixty-five days and a quarter

---

XVI. [1] They also showed me the other arrangement, that of the moon, B.   [2] And all its course. And the men showed me all the movements of these two, B; A om.   [3] A Sok. om.   [4] Eternal, B. [5] Towards the East, B.   [6] B om.   [7] B OMITS ENTIRE VERSE. Sok. reads the first gates (western place of the sun) 31 days to the place of the sun exactly. For 31 A reads 1.   [8] Emended from 35 A Sok.   [9] 35, A.   [10] 31, Sok.   [11] 22, Sok.   [12] Sok. adds in the days.

XVI. 1. **Twelve great gates.** These are the same as the gates of the sun in xiii.   2–3. It is obvious that the text is here corrupt, as this account cannot possibly apply to the moon. In order to correct it we have only to read 'sun' instead of 'moon' wherever it occurs. We have thus a description of the Solar year. The numbers when added together = 365. Hence in ver. 4 we are told that a Solar year = 365¼ days. Then in ver. 5 we proceed to consider the lunar year which amounts not to 365 but to 354 days, there being a difference of eleven days, or more exactly eleven and a quarter days.

of one day [1].   5. But in the lunar year there are three
hundred and fifty-four days, making twelve months of twenty-
nine days; and * there remain eleven days over, which belong
to the solar circle of the whole year [2], and are * lunar epacts
of the whole year [3]. [Thus the great circle has five hundred
and thirty-two years.]   6. The fourth part (of one day) is
neglected during three years and the fourth year completes it
exactly.   * On account of this they are omitted from the
heavens during three years, and are not added to the number
of the days [4], on which account these change the seasons of
the year * in two new months, to make the number complete
and there are two others to diminish [5].   7. And when she
has gone through the Western gates, she returns and goes to
the Eastern, with her light, * and so she goes day and night
in the heavenly circles, below all the circles more quickly than

---

[1] So she sets by the western gates and finishes the year in 364
days that are accomplished, B. This may be the original text, or 364 may
be an error for 354. B OMITS VERSE 5.   [2] Eleven days of the solar
circle are wanting, Sok.   [3] Epacts of the lunar year, A.   [4] She
goes through the year on this account and therefore the computation
is made apart from the heavens, and in the years the days are not
reckoned, B.   [5] B om.

XVI. 5. **Twenty-nine days.** This
should be 'twenty-nine and a half
days.' [Thus the great circle has
532 years.] I have bracketed these
words as they have no real connexion
with the context. They arose obviously
from a marginal gloss. The writer in
this chapter does not get beyond
the Metonic cycle, whereas the great
cycle of 532 years is produced by
multiplying together the Metonic
cycle of nineteen years, and the Solar
cycle of twenty-eight years. This
great cycle is called the Dionysian or
Great Paschal Period. As it includes
all the variations in respect of the
new moons and the dominical letters,
it is consequently a period in which
Easter and all the movable and un-
movable feasts would occur on the
same day of the week and month as
in the corresponding year of the preceding cycle. This cycle was first
proposed by Victorius of Aquitaine,
circ. 457 A. D. It is obvious that any
reference to such a cycle here is an
intrusion.   6. **The fourth part,
&c.** Explanation of leap year. **On
which account these change the
seasons of the year, &c.** Hopelessly corrupt.   7. **With her
light.** This seems to imply that her
light is not borrowed from the sun
as it is taught in the Eth. En. lxxiii.

the winds of the heavens, and there are spirits and creatures, and angels flying[1], with six wings to each of the angels[2]. 8. * And seven (months) are computed to the circle of the moon during a revolution of nineteen years[3].

[*Of the singing of the Angels, which cannot be described.*]

XVII. 1. In the middle of the heavens I saw an armed host serving the Lord with cymbals, and organs, and unceasing voice[4]. I was delighted at hearing it.

[*Of the taking up of Enoch into the fifth Heaven.*]

XVIII. 1. The men took * and brought[5] me up into the fifth heaven[6], and I saw there many hosts * not to be counted

---

[1] So Sok. but that it omits of the heavens and of the angels. B reads, So their circle goes as it were round the heavens and their chariot. The wind goes with it, urging its course and the flying spirits draw on the chariots.   [2] B adds and such is the arrangement of the moon. [3] So Sok.; and its course is in seven different directions for nineteen years, A ; B om.

XVII. [4] A adds and noble and continuous and varied singing, which it is not possible to describe. And so wonderful and strange is the singing of these angels that it amazes every mind. Sok. adds and with noble singing.

XVIII. [5] A B om.   A[6] adds and placed me there.

Spirits . . . with six wings. The moon has its attendant *six-winged* spirits as the sun has its *twelve-winged* attendants (xii. 2). 8. This verse deals with the Metonic cycle. This cycle consists of a period of nineteen solar years, after which the new moons happen on the same days of the year. As nineteen solar years = 6,939·1860 days = 235 lunar months = nineteen lunar years and seven months, the solar and lunar years can be reconciled by intercalating seven lunar months at the close of the 3rd, 5th, 8th, 11th, 13th, 16th, and 19th years of the cycle.

XVII. An armed host. The

purpose for which they are armed is given in Test. Levi 3, though in this Testament they are placed in the third heaven: ἐν τῷ τρίτῳ εἰσὶν αἱ δυνάμεις τῶν παρεμβολῶν, οἱ ταχθέντες εἰς ἡμέραν κρίσεως, ποιῆσαι ἐκδίκησιν ἐν τοῖς πνεύμασι τῆς πλάνης καὶ τοῦ Βελίαρ.   Serving the Lord with cymbals . . . and unceasing voice. This is exactly the conception which Test. Levi 3 gives of the functions of the inhabitants of the fourth heaven: ἐν δὲ τῷ μετ' αὐτὸν εἰσὶ θρόνοι, ἐξουσίαι, ἐν ᾧ ὕμνοι ἀεὶ τῷ θεῷ προσφέρονται.

XVIII. 1. Fifth heaven. Our text and Test. Levi 3 differ absolutely called Grigori [1]; and their appearance was like men, and their size was * greater than that of the giants [2]. 2. And their countenances were withered, and their lips are always silent. And there was no service in * the fifth [3] heaven. And I said to the men who were with me : ' Why are these men very withered, and their faces melancholy, and their lips silent, and there is no service in this heaven ? ' 3. And they said to me : ' These are the Grigori, who, with their prince Satanail,

---

[1] B om. [2] **Greater than great wonders, B. Great and they were huge limbed, A.** B OM. REST OF CHAPTER. [3] This, Sok.

---

as to the inhabitants of the fifth heaven. According to the latter the inhabitants are οἱ ἄγγελοι οἱ φέροντες τὰς ἀποκρίσεις τοῖς ἀγγέλοις τοῦ προσώπου κυρίου. This view, however, seems limited to the Test. of Levi, whereas we find in *Chag.* 12[b] the same view expressed as here: i. e. in מען the fifth heaven are to be found ' hosts of angels praising God by night, but keeping silent by day that God may hear the praises of Israel.' The latter clause is a late Rabbinic idea. Again, in Clem. Alex. *Strom.* v. 11. 77, we find a fragment of the Apocalypse of Zephaniah which supports, and in all probability is based on, our text : ἆρ' οὐχ ὅμοια ταῦτα τοῖς ὑπὸ Σοφονία λεχθεῖσι τοῦ προφήτου; καὶ ἀνέλαβέν με πνεῦμα καὶ ἀνήνεγκέν με εἰς οὐρανὸν πέμπτον καὶ ἐθεώρουν ἀγγέλους καλουμένους κυρίους . . . ὑμνοῦντας θεὸν ἄρρητον ὕψιστον. This Apocalypse is extant in Thebaic in a fragmentary condition, but these fragments do not contain the passage just quoted. **Grigori.** These are the Watchers, the Ἐγρήγοροι, or עירים, of whom we have so full accounts in the Eth. En. vi–xvi.; xix.; lxxxvi. **3. The Grigori.** These are the angels whose brethren rebelled and

were confined in the second heaven. See vi. 3 (note). These Watchers rebelled against God before the angels were tempted to sin with the daughters of men. In other words, we have here the agents of the original revolt in heaven, the Satans; and their leader is naturally named Satanail. These existed as evil agencies before the fall of the angels; for in Eth. En. liv. 6 the guilt of the latter consisted in becoming subject to Satan. See Eth. En. xl. 7 (note). The myth here, however, varies somewhat from that in Eth. En. vi–xvi. The leaders in the Eth. En. vi–xvi. are not Satans, but ' watchers,' like their followers. In Eth. En. lxix, however, we have an account which harmonizes with our text. There we see that the superior angels had rebelled before the creation of Adam; that they had tempted Eve and brought about the fall of the angels in the days of Jared. Thus, in Eth. En. lxix. and here, the leaders of the angels who fell in Jared's days are Satans. This is practically the view of portions of the Talmud. See Weber, pp. 211, 243, 244. **Who with their prince Satanail.** Quoted in Test. Dan. 5 . . τῶν πνευμάτων τῆς πλάνης. Ἀνέγνων

rejected the holy[1] Lord[2].   4. And *in consequence of these
things [3] they are kept in great darkness in the second heaven ;
* and of them there went three [4] to the earth from the throne
of God to the place Ermon ; and they entered into dealings
on the side of Mount Iermon, and they saw the daughters
of men, that they were fair, and took unto themselves wives.
5. And they made the earth foul with their deeds [5]. And
they acted lawlessly in all times of this age, and wrought
confusion, and the giants were born, and the strangely tall
men, and there was much wickedness.   6. And on account
of this God judged them with a mighty judgement. And
they lament for their brethren, and they will be punished at
the great day of the Lord.   7. And I said to the Grigori :
' I have seen your brethren and their works, and their great [1]

---

[1] Sok. om.   [2] Sok. adds to the number of twenty millions.   [3] Those
who followed them are the prisoners who, Sok.   [4] Who went, Sok.
[5] Sok. adds And the wives of men continue to do evil.

γὰρ ἐν βίβλῳ Ἐνὼχ τοῦ δικαίου, ὅτι
ὁ ἄρχων ὑμῶν ἐστὶν ὁ Σατανᾶς. ὑμῶν
is here corrupt for αὐτῶν. The text
cannot mean that all the watchers
rebelled, but only that it was from
the class of the watchers that the
rebels proceeded. It is, of course,
just possible that the writers' scheme
may differ from the conception we
have given above, and be as follows.
The rebellious watchers, with their
prince Satanail, are confined to the
fifth heaven. The subordinate angels
who followed them are imprisoned
in the second heaven, whereas the
watchers who went down to earth and
sinned with women are imprisoned
under the earth. This view is very
attractive, but is open to more difficulties of interpretation than the one
we have followed. The MSS. reading
fifth in vii. 3 is indeed in its favour,
but then for ' prince and ' in the
same verse we must read ' prince and
leaders who.' The main objections
to this interpretation, however, lie
in xviii. 8, 9, and in vii. 3, where the
prisoners of the second heaven are
clearly identified with the watchers.
In xxx. 1-3 Satanail with his angels
is cast down from heaven.   4.
Kept . . . in the second heaven :
see vii. 3.   **Three.** According to
Eth. En. ix. 6 Azazel, or vi. 3, ix. 7
Semjaza : according to *Jalkut* Schim.,
Beresch 44 Assael and Semjaza.
Ermon : see Eth. En. vi. 2-6 (notes).
**Entered into dealings on . . .
Mount Iermon** : Eth. En. vi. 5.
5. Eth. En. x. 8 ; vii. 2.   **6.** Eth.
En. x. 4-15. **They will be punished** :
i. e. the lustful watchers.   **7.** There
is a confusion in this verse. In vii.
Enoch has seen the rebellious
watchers being tortured in the second
heaven ; whereas he says here that he

torments[1]. And I have prayed for them, but God has condemned them (to be) under the earth, till the heaven and
earth are ended for ever.'   . 8. And I said: ' Why do ye
* wait, brethren[2], and not serve before the face of the Lord?
and perform your duties[3] before the face of the Lord, and do
not anger your Lord[4] to the end.'   9. And they listened
to my rebuke. And they * stood in the four orders in this[5]
heaven, and lo! as I was standing with these men, four
trumpets resounded together with a loud voice, and the
Grigori sang with one voice, and their voices went forth
before the Lord[6] with sadness and tenderness.

[The taking up of Enoch into the sixth Heaven.]

XIX. 1. And these men took me thence and brought me
to the sixth heaven, and I saw there seven bands of angels,
very bright and glorious, and their faces shining more than
* the rays of[7] the sun. * They are resplendent[7], and there
is no difference * in their countenances, or their manner, or
the style of their clothing[8].   2. *And these orders[9] arrange
and study * the revolutions of the stars, and the changes

---

[1] Sok. adds **and their great entreaties**.   [2] **Await your brethren**,
Sok.   [3] Sok. adds **and serve**.   [4] Sok. adds **your God**.   [5] **Spoke to
the four orders in**, A.   [6] Sok. adds **God**.
    XIX. [7] B om.   [8] **Of form between them nor in the fashion of their
raiment**, Sok.   [9] **Some of these angels**, B.

---

has seen the lustful watchers who are
punished under the earth. I have
prayed for them: cf. vii. 5 (note).
8, 9. The watchers are silent out
of sympathy with their brethren
who are punished in the second
heaven and under the earth, but at
Enoch's rebuke they resume the worship they had left off. Even so their
singing is still marked with sadness.
    XIX. 1. The account of the sixth
heaven disagrees more or less with
that of Test. Levi 3, with that of

Chag. 12[b], and with the colourless
account in the Asc. Is. There is no
difference in their countenances,
&c.: Asc. Is. viii. 16 'Omnium una
species et gloria aequalis,' seems to be
derived from our text, as it emphasizes the differences in glory between
the angelic orders in each of the first
five heavens, and emphasizes no less
the equality in glory of all the angels
of the sixth heaven (cf. Asc. Is. viii.
5–7).   **2.** The heavenly bodies are
under Uriel in Eth. En. lxxii–lxxxii.

of the moon, and revolutions of the sun, and superintend the good or evil condition of the world [1].   3. *And they [2] arrange teachings, and instructions, and sweet * speaking, and [3] singing, and all * kinds of glorious [4] praise.   * These are the archangels who are appointed over the angels ! They hold in subjection all living things both in heaven and earth [5]. 4. And there are the angels who are over seasons and years, and the angels who are over rivers and the sea, and those who are over the fruits * of the earth, and the angels over every herb, giving all kinds of nourishment to every living thing [6].   5. And the angels over all souls of men, who write down all their works and their lives [7] before the face of the Lord.   6. In the midst of them are seven phoenixes and seven cherubims, and seven six-winged creatures, * being as one voice and singing with one voice [8]; and it is not possible to describe their singing, and * they rejoice before the Lord [9] at His footstool.

[*Thence Enoch is taken into the seventh Heaven* [10].]

XX. 1. And these men took me thence *and brought me [11]

---

[1] The peaceful order of the world, and the revolutions of the sun, moon, and stars.   [2] Other heavenly angels, B.   [3] And clear, A ; voiced, Sok.   [4] Things concerned with, A.   [5] So A Sok.; but that A reads measure for hold in subjection, B om.   [6] So A Sok.; but that A reads all those who give nourishment for giving all kinds of nourishment; B reads and grass and all things that grow.   [7] And the angels who write down all the souls of men and all their works and their lives, A ; Other angels arrange the things of all men and all living things, and write, B.   [8] With one voice they sing in harmony, A ; Each uttering words by himself, and singing by himself things in harmony, B. [9] The Lord rejoices with them, B.

XX. [10] Entry of Enoch into the seventh heaven, B.   [11] A om.

---

4. In Eth. En. lx. it is subordinate spirits that are over these natural objects. Cf. Eth. En. lxxxii. 13 ; Rev. ix. 14 ; xvi. 5.   5. It is Raphael in Eth. En. xx. 3.   6. Six-winged creatures : i. e. seraphim. Cf. xii. 1 (notes). Observe that both cherubim and seraphim are also in the seventh heaven. *Chag.* 12[b] places the Sera-

phim, Ophannim, and Chajjoth, and other angels of service in the seventh heaven. Test. Levi 3 in agreement with this verse represents the inhabitants of the sixth heaven as οἱ ἄγγελοί εἰσι τοῦ προσώπου κυρίου, οἱ λειτουργοῦντες.

XX. 1. With this description of the heavenly hosts cf. Is. vi ; Ezek.

to the seventh heaven, and I saw there a very [1] great light and
*all the fiery hosts of great archangels, and incorporeal powers [2]
* and lordships, and principalities, and powers ; cherubim
and seraphim, thrones [1] * and the watchfulness of many eyes.
There were ten troops, a station of brightness [3], and I was
afraid, and trembled * with a great terror [1].   2. And those
men * took hold of me and brought me into their midst [4]
and said to me : ' Be of good cheer, Enoch, be not afraid.'
3. And they showed me the Lord from afar sitting on His
lofty [5] throne [6]. And all the heavenly hosts having approached
stood [1] on the ten [1] steps, * according to their rank : and [1] made

---

[1] B om.   [2] A fiery host of great archangels of spiritual forms, A.
All the fiery and bright host of the incorporeal archangels, B.   [3] And
the ten many-eyed bands of bright station, Sok. ; B om. After brightness
A Sok. add the gloss like the followers of John. For nine (A) I have
read ten with Sok.   [4] Placed me in their midst, B. For unto their
midst A reads after them.   [5] Very lofty, Sok., B om.   [6] A adds for
it is that upon which God rests. In the tenth heaven, in the tenth
heaven is God. In the Hebrew language it is called Avarat.

---

i ; Eth. En. xiv. 9-17 ; lxxi. 7-9 ;
Rev. iv. For *Chag.* 12ᵇ see xix. 6
(note). But this account can well
compare for grandeur with any of the
above. Lordships, and principalities, and powers . . . thrones. So
exactly Col. i. 16 εἴτε θρόνοι εἴτε κυριότητες εἴτε ἀρχαὶ εἴτε ἐξουσίαι.   Cf.
Eph. i. 21 ἀρχῆς καὶ ἐξουσίας καὶ δυνά-
μεως καὶ κυριότητος : also Rom. viii.
38 ; Eph. iii. 10, 15 ; 1 Pet. iii. 22 ;
Eth. En. lxi. 10. Watchfulness of
many eyes seems to be derived from
Ezek. x. 12. These are the Ophannim, Eth. En. lxi. 10.   Ten . . .
brightness. These are the ten orders
of angels mentioned in ver. 3.   Was
afraid and trembled : Eth. En. xiv.
14.   2. Be of good cheer, &c. :
cf. i. 8.   3. The Lord . . . on
His lofty throne : Is. vi. 1 ; Eth.
En. xiv. 20 ; Rev. xix. 4. All the
heavenly hosts . . . on the ten
steps according to their rank.

These hosts consist of the ten troops
mentioned in ver. 1, arranged in the
order of their rank. According to
Maimonides in the *Mishne Thora*
S. 1 ; Jesode Thora C. 2, they are :
Chajjoth, Ophannim, Arellim, Chash-
mallim, Seraphim, Mal'achim, Elohim,
Bene Elohim, Kerubim, Ishim (Weber, p. 163). In the *Berith menucha*
the list is different : Arellim, Ishim,
Bene Elohim, Mal'achim, Chashmal-
lim, Tarshishim, Shina'nim, Kerubim,
Ophannim, Seraphim (Eisenmenger,
ii. 374). But the nearest parallel is
to be found in the nine orders of Dionysius the Areopagite, i. e. Σεραφίμ,
Χερουβίμ, Θρόνοι, Κυριότητες, Δυνάμεις, Ἐξουσίαι, Ἀρχαί, Ἀρχάγγελοι,
Ἄγγελοι. These are reproduced in
Dante, *Par.* c. xxviii, where the
slightly differing arrangement of
Gregory the Great (*Hom.* xxxiv. 7)
is censured.

obeisance to the Lord.　　4. And so they proceeded to their places in joy and mirth, and in boundless light * singing songs with low and gentle voices [1], * and gloriously serving Him [2].

[*How the Angels placed Enoch there at the limits of the seventh Heaven, and departed from him invisibly.*]

XXI. 1. They leave not * nor depart day or night [3] standing before the face of the Lord, working His will [4], cherubim and seraphim, standing round His throne. * And the six-winged creatures [5] overshadow all [6] His throne, singing * with a soft voice [6] before the face of the Lord : * 'Holy, Holy, Holy: Lord God of Sabaoth! heaven and earth are full of Thy glory [6]!'　　2. When I had seen all these things, * these men said unto me : 'Enoch, up to this time we have been ordered to accompany thee.' And [6] those men departed from me, and I saw them no more. And I remained alone at the extremity of the heaven [7], and was afraid, and fell on my face, * and said within myself: 'Woe is me! what has come upon me ! [8].'　　3. And the Lord sent one of His glorious archangels [6], Gabriel, and he said to me : 'Be of good cheer, Enoch, * be not afraid [9], * stand up, come with me [10], and stand up before the face of the Lord for ever.　　4. And I answered him, * and said [11]: 'Oh! Lord, my spirit has departed from me with fear * and trembling [6]! * call to me the men [12] who have brought me to this place : upon them

---

[1] B om.　　[2] The glorious ones seeing Him, Suk.
XXI. [3] A om.　　[4] B adds and the whole host of.　　[5] With six wings and many eyes, A.　　[6] B om.　　[7] Seventh heaven, A.　　[8] B om.　　[9] Fear not thou these hosts, B.　　[10] Come unto me, B. A transposes these words after for ever.　　[11] B om.; A adds within myself. B adds Woe is me, O Lord !　　[12] I called the men, A B.

XXI. 1. **Leave not nor depart day or night.** This is derived from Eth. En. xiv. 23 'The holy ones of the holy—leave not by night nor depart.' 'Six-winged creatures . . . Holy, holy, holy, &c.,' Is. vi. 2, 3.
3. **Be of good cheer, be not afraid.** See i. 8; xx. 2; xxi. 5; Eth. En.

I have relied, and with them I would go before the face of the Lord.'   5. And Gabriel hurried me away like a leaf carried off by the wind, * and he took me [1] and set me before the face of the Lord [2].

XXII. 4. I fell down [3] and worshipped the Lord.   5. And the Lord spake with His lips to me: ' Be of good cheer,

---

[1] Having taken me, Sok., A om.   [2] A adds 6. And I saw the eighth heaven, which is called in the Hebrew language, Muzaloth, changing in its season in dryness and moisture, with the twelve signs of the zodiac, which are above the seventh heaven. And I saw the ninth heaven, which in the Hebrew is called Kukhavim, where are the heavenly homes of the twelve signs of the zodiac.

Michael the Archangel led Enoch into the tenth heaven before the face of the Lord.

XXII. 1. In the tenth heaven Aravoth, I saw the vision of the face of the Lord, like iron burnt in the fire, and brought forth and emitting sparks, and it burns. So I saw the face of the Lord; but the face of the Lord cannot be told. It is wonderful and awful, and very terrible. 2. And who am I that I should tell of the unspeakable being of God, and His wonderful face? And it is not for me to tell of His wonderful knowledge and various utterances ; and the very great throne of the Lord not made with hands. And how many stand around Him, hosts of cherubim and seraphim.   3. And moreover their never-ceasing songs, and their unchanging beauty, and the unspeakable greatness of His beauty, who can tell ?

In Sok. a duplicate, but somewhat different, version of XXII. 1–3 is given :—

I also saw the Lord face to face. And His face was very glorious, marvellous and terrible, threatening, and strange.   2. Who am I to tell of the incomprehensible existence of the Lord, and His face wonderful, and not to be spoken of : and the choir with much instruction, and loud sound, and the throne of the Lord very great, and not made with hands : and the choir standing around Him of the hosts of cherubim and seraphim !

[3] B adds and could not see the Lord God.

---

xv. 1.   5. Cf. ver. 3.   [6. This verse is clearly an interpolation. It is not found either in B or Sok. Furthermore, throughout the rest of the book only seven heavens are mentioned or implied. The term Muzaloth is the Hebrew name for the twelve signs of the Zodiac מַזָּלוֹת. Kukhavim is merely a transliteration of כּוֹכָבִים. Some ground for this conception may be found in Eth. En.

xiv. 17, where the path of the stars is above the throne of God, and as the throne of God according to this book is in the seventh heaven, the signs and stars might be regarded as in the eighth or ninth.]

XXII. [1–3. Aravoth a transliteration of ערבות, which according to *Chagig* 12[b] was really the seventh heaven. The rest of ver. 1 and verses 2, 3, may in some form have belonged

Enoch, be not afraid: rise up and stand before my face for
ever.'   6. And Michael, the chief captain, * lifted me up,
and [1] brought me before the face of the Lord, and the Lord
said to His servants making trial of them : ' Let Enoch come
to stand before My face for ever!'   7. And the glorious
ones made obeisance * to the Lord, and said: ' Let Enoch
proceed according to Thy word [2] !'   8. And the Lord said
to Michael: '* Go and take from Enoch his earthly robe,
and anoint him with My holy [3] oil, and clothe him with the
raiment of My glory.'   9. And so Michael * did as the
Lord spake unto him. He [4] anointed me [5] and clothed me,
and the appearance of that oil was more than a great light,
and its anointing was like excellent dew ; and its fragrance
like myrrh, shining like a ray of the sun.   10. * And
I gazed upon myself, and I was like one of His glorious
ones [6].   * And there was no difference, and fear and
trembling departed from me [7].   11. And the Lord called
one of His archangels, by name Vretil [8], who * was more wise
than the other archangels, and [9] wrote down all the doings of
the Lord.   12. And the Lord said to Vretil [8], ' Bring forth

---

[1] B om. and transposes verses 8–10 before 5.   [2] And told me to come
forth, B.   [3] **Take Enoch and strip from him all earthly things and
anoint him with fine,** B.   [4] **Stripped me of my clothes and,** B.
[5] **With blessed oil,** B.   [6] Sok. om.   [7] A Sok. om.   [8] Pravuil, A ;
Vrevoil, Sok.   [9] **With wisdom,** B.

---

to the text. I have with some hesi-
tation rejected them].   **6. Michael.**
Cf. Eth. En. lxxi. 13, 14, where
Michael takes charge of Enoch. He
is likewise the chief of the archangels,
Eth. En. xl. 9. As being the angel
set over Israel, Eth. En. xx. 5, he is
naturally the chief captain.   **8.**
This is τὸ ἔλαιον τοῦ ἐλέου of *Apoc.
Mosis* ed. Tischend. p. 6.   **Holy oil.**
See viii. 7: Evang. Nicod. ii. 3.
This oil is described in ver. 9, and its
effects in ver. 10.   **Raiment of my
glory.** These are the garments of

the blessed. Cf. Eth. En. lxii. 15 ;
cviii. 12 ; 2 Cor. v. 3, 4 ; Rev. iii. 4,
5, 18 ; iv. 4 ; vi. 11 ; vii. 9, 13, 14 ;
4 Ezra ii. 39, 45 ; Herm. *Sim.* viii.
2 ; Asc. Is. ix. 9.   **11. Vretil.** I
cannot find this name anywhere else.
12. Give a reed to Enoch. These
words are drawn upon in *Liber S.
Joannis Apocryphus* (Thilo, *Cod.
Apocr. N. T.* vol. i. p. 890) ' Ele-
vavit Henoc super firmamentum . . .
et praecepit ei dari calamum . . .
et sedens scripsit sexaginta septem
libros.

the books from my store-places, * and give a reed to Enoch [1], * and interpret to him the books [2].'   * And Vretil made haste and brought me the books, fragrant with myrrh, and gave me a reed from his hand [3].

[*Of the Writing of Enoch how he wrote about his wonderful Goings and the heavenly Visions, and he himself wrote 366 Books.*]

XXIII. 1. And he told me all the works of * the heaven and [4] the earth and the sea, * and their goings and comings [5], * the noise of the thunder; the sun and moon and the movement of the stars; their changings; the seasons and years; days and hours [6]; and [7] goings of the winds; and the numbers of the angels; * the songs of the armed hosts [8].   2. And everything relating to man, and every language of their songs, and the lives of men, and the precepts [9] and instructions, and sweet-voiced singings, and all which it is suitable to be instructed in.   3. * And Vretil instructed me thirty days and thirty nights, and his lips never ceased speaking; and I did not cease thirty days and thirty nights writing all the remarks [10].   4. And Vretil [11] said to me: * 'All the things which I have told thee, thou hast written down.   Sit [12] down and * write all about [13] the souls

---

[1] And take a reed for speedy writing and give it to Enoch, A Sok.
[2] A om.   [3] And show him the books wonderful and fragrant with myrrh from thy hand, A; Sok. agrees with text, save that he adds wonderful before books, and adds for speedy writing after reed.
XXIII. [4] B om.   [5] The movements of all the elements, B; A om.
[6] The living things and the seasons of the year, and the course of his days and their changings, and the teaching of the commandments, B; Sok. supports text, save that for movement of the stars he reads stars and their goings. After hours Sok. adds and the coming forth of the clouds.
[7] B OMITS from and goings to end of ver. 2.   [8] The fashion of their songs, A.   [9] Narratives, A.   [10] A om.; Sok. supports text, but that for remarks he reads marks of every creature. After creature Sok. adds and when I had finished the thirty days and nights.   [11] Právuil, A; Vrevoil, Sok. So also in previous verse.   [12] Lo! what things I have instructed thee in and what thou hast written: and now sit, Sok.
[13] Write down all, Sok.

XXIII. 1. This verse would not unsuitably describe the Book of Celes- tial Physics in Eth. En. lxxii–lxxxii. Songs of the armed hosts: see xvii.

of men, those of them which are not born, and the places prepared for them for ever.   5. For every soul was created eternally [1] before the foundation of the world.'   6. And I * wrote all out continuously [2] during thirty days and thirty nights, * and I copied all out accurately, and I wrote 366 books [3].

---

[1] For eternity, Sok.   [2] Sat, Sok.   [3] And so I ceased and I had written 360 books, B.

---

5. Every soul was created . . . before the foundation of the world. The Platonic doctrine of the pre-existence of the soul is here taught. We find that it had already made its way into Jewish thought in Egypt; cf. *Wisdom of Solomon*, viii. 19, 20 παῖς δὲ ἤμην εὐφυής, ψυχῆς τε ἔλαχον ἀγαθῆς, μᾶλλον δὲ ἀγαθὸς ὢν ἦλθον εἰς σῶμα ἀμίαντον. This doctrine was accepted and further developed by Philo. According to him the whole atmosphere is filled with souls. Among these, those who are nearer the earth and are attracted by the body descend into mortal bodies (τούτων τῶν ψυχῶν αἱ μὲν κάτιασιν ἐνδεθησόμεναι σώμασι θνητοῖς, ὅσαι προσγειόταται καὶ φιλοσώματοι, *De Somn.* i. 22). When they have entered the body they are swept off by it as by a river and swallowed up in its eddies (ἐκεῖναι δὲ ὥσπερ εἰς ποταμὸν τὸ σῶμα καταβᾶσαι τοτὲ μὲν ὑπὸ συρμοῦ δίνης βιαιοτάτης ἁρπασθεῖσαι κατεπόθησαν, *De Gigant.* 3). Only a few escape by obedience to a spiritual philosophy and come to share in the incorporeal and imperishable life that is with God (*De Gigant.* 3). But there were other souls, called demons in philosophy and angels in Scripture, who dwelling in the higher parts are never entangled by love of the earthly (μηδενὸς μὲν τῶν περιγείων ποτὲ ὀρεχθεῖσαι τὸ παράπαν, *De Somn.* i. 22), and

who reported the commands of the Father to the children, and the needs of the children to the Father (τὰς τοῦ πατρὸς ἐπικελεύσεις τοῖς ἐκγόνοις καὶ τὰς τῶν ἐκγόνων χρείας τῷ πατρὶ διαγγέλλουσι, *De Somn.* i. 22 ; cf. *De Gigant.* 4). This doctrine of the preexistence of the soul was according to Josephus, *Bell. Jud.* ii. 8. 11, held by the Essenes : καὶ γὰρ ἔρρωται παρ' αὐτοῖς ἥδε ἡ δόξα, φθαρτὰ μὲν εἶναι τὰ σώματα καὶ τὴν ὕλην οὐ μόνιμον αὐτοῖς, τὰς δὲ ψυχὰς ἀθανάτους ἀεὶ διαμένειν, καὶ συμπλέκεσθαι μέν, ἐκ τοῦ λεπτοτάτου φοιτώσας αἰθέρος, ὥσπερ εἱρκταῖς τοῖς σώμασιν ἴυγγί τινι φυσικῇ κατασπωμένας, ἐπειδὰν δὲ ἀνεθῶσι τῶν κατὰ σάρκα δεσμῶν, οἷα δὴ μακρᾶς δουλείας ἀπηλλαγμένας, τότε χαίρειν καὶ μετεώρους φέρεσθαι. It became a prevailing dogma in later Judaism. All souls which were to enter human bodies existed before the creation of the world in the Garden of Eden (*Tanchuma*, Pikkude 3) or in the seventh heaven (*Chagig* 12[b]) or in a certain chamber (אוצר) (*Sifre* 143[b]) whence God called them forth to enter human bodies. These souls were conceived of as actually living beings. According to *Bereshith rabba* c. 8, God takes counsel with the souls of the righteous before He creates the earth (cf. Weber, pp. 204, 205, 217-220). See xxx. 16 (note).

[*Of the great Secrets of God, which God revealed and told to Enoch, and spoke with him Face to Face.*]

XXIV. 1. And the Lord called me * and said to me : ‘ Enoch, sit thou on My [1] left hand with Gabriel.’ And I made obeisance to the Lord.   2. And the Lord spake to me : ‘ Enoch [2], * the things which thou seest at rest and in motion were completed by me [3]. I will tell thee * now, even [4] from the first, what things I created from the non-existent, and what visible things from the invisible [5].   3. Not even to My angels have I told My secrets, nor have I informed them of * their origin, nor have they understood My infinite creation [6] which I tell thee of to-day.   4. * For before anything which is visible existed [7], * I alone held my course among the invisible things [8], like the sun from the east to the west, * and from the west to the east.   5. But even the sun has rest in himself, but I did not find rest,

---

XXIV. [1] And placed me on His, B.   [2] Beloved Enoch, A.   [3] Thou seest the things which are now completed, A.   [4] All, Sok.   [5] A adds Listen Enoch and pay attention to these words, for.   [6] Their origin nor of My infinite empire, nor have they understood the creation made by Me, A.   My mysteries nor their explanations nor My boundless and inexplicable plans in creation, B.   [7] B om.   [8] I revealed the light: I went about in the light as one of the invisible.

XXIV. 2. From the non-existent. Here creation *ex nihilo* seems to be taught. In Philo, on the other hand, the world was not created, but only formed from pre-existent chaotic elements. In one passage, however, where the absolute creation of the world is taught, we have an actual and almost verbal agreement with our text—ὡς ἥλιος ἀνατείλας τὰ κεκρυμμένα τῶν σωμάτων ἐπιδείκνυται, οὕτω καὶ ὁ θεὸς τὰ πάντα γεννήσας οὐ μόνον εἰς τὸ ἐμφανὲς ἤγαγεν, ἀλλὰ καὶ ἃ πρότερον οὐκ ἦν ἐποίησεν, οὐ δημιουργὸς μόνον, ἀλλὰ καὶ κτίστης αὐτὸς ὤν (*De Somn.* i. 13). Probably, however, from the non-existent is a rendering of ἐκ τῶν μὴ ὄντων. This will harmonize with xxv. 1. Visible things from the invisible : cf. passage just quoted from Philo; also Heb. xi. 3 ‘The worlds have been formed by the word of God, so that what is seen hath not been made out of things which do appear.’ These words from *Hebrews* do not necessarily imply creation, but can naturally be interpreted after Philo's conceptions.   In Gen. i. 2 LXX we find the idea of invisible elements introduced, as it gives ἡ δὲ γῆ ἦν ἀόρατος as a rendering of what we translate with ‘the earth was waste.’   3. Not even to My angels : cf. xl. 3 ; 1 Pet. i. 12.

because I was creating every thing[1]. And I planned to lay the foundations and to make the visible creation.

[*God tells Enoch how out of the lowest Darkness, there comes forth the visible and the invisible.*]

XXV. 1. '*And I commanded in the depths that visible things should come out of invisible. And out came Adoil very great[2], *and I gazed upon him. And lo! his colour was red, of great brightness[3].   2. And I said unto him: "Burst asunder, Adoil[4], and let that which comes from thee be visible."   3. And he burst asunder, and there came forth a great light[5], and *I was in the midst of a great light, and as the light came forth from the light[6], there came forth the great world, *revealing all the creation[3], which I had purposed to make, and I saw that it was good.   4. And I made for Myself a throne, and sat upon it, and I said to the light:

---

[1] B om.
   XXV. [2] I summoned from the regions below the great Idoil to come forth who had in his belly a great stone, B.   [3] B om.   [4] A om.
[5] Stone, B.   [6] I was in the midst of light, and the light thus appearing out of it, Sok.; B om.

XXV. 1. Here the formation of the world from pre-existing elements is taught, as in the Book of Wisdom xi. 17 ἐξ ἀμόρφου ὕλης. Cf. also Philo, *De Justitia* 7 Μηνύει δὲ ἡ τοῦ Κόσμου γένεσις ... τὰ γὰρ μὴ ὄντα ἐκάλεσεν εἰς τὸ εἶναι. This is in the main the teaching of the Talmud. See Weber, 193–196. Adoil. Is this from יד אל, the hand of God? The word does not occur elsewhere that I am aware of. In this and the two subsequent verses we have an adaptation of an Egyptian myth.   2. We have here a modification of the egg theory of the universe. See Clem. *Recog.* x. 17, 30. In Brugsch, *Rel. u. Myth. d. alten Aegypter*, p. 101, we find a very close parallel. According to the monuments: 'der erste Schöpfungsact began

mit der Bildung eines Eies aus dem Urgewässer, aus dem das Tageslicht, die unmittelbare Ursache des Lebens in dem Bereiche der irdischen Welt herausbrach.'   3. There came forth a great light. This exactly agrees with the ancient Egyptian myth as described in preceding note. Cf. also Brugsch, *Rel. u. Myth.* pp. 160, 161 on *Die Geburt des Lichtes*. There came forth the great world. This should refer to the world of the heavens, as the earth is dealt with in the next chapter.   4. I made for Myself a throne. This throne was created before the world according to *Bereshith rabba* c. 1 as here. This idea may have found support in the LXX of Prov. viii. 27, where wisdom declares that she was with

" Go forth * on high [1] and be established above My throne [2], and be the foundation for things on high.'   5. And there was nothing higher than the light, and as I reclined, I saw it from My throne.

[*God again calls from the Depths and there came forth Arkhas, Tazhis* [3], *and one who is very red.*]

XXVI. 1. And I summoned a second time from the depths, *and said: ' Let the solid thing which is visible come forth from the invisible [4].' And Arkhas * came forth [5] firm [6] and heavy [3] and * very red [7].   2. And I said : ' Be thou divided, O Arkhas, and let * that be seen which is [8] produced from thee.' And when he was divided, the world came forth, very dark and great, * bringing the creation of all things below [9].   3. And I saw that it [10] was good. And I said to him : ' * Go thou down [11] and be thou established. *And be a foundation for things below'; and it was so. And it came forth and was established [12], and was a foundation for things below. * And there was nothing else below the darkness [12].

[*How God established the Water, and surrounded it with Light, and established upon it Seven Islands.*]

XXVII. 1. * And I ordered that there should be a separation between the light and the darkness, and I said : ' Let

---

[1] **Above My throne,** Sok.   [2] Sok. om.
XXVI. [3] Corrupt in A, from тяжесть = heaviness (Old Slav.).   [4] I told him to come forth from the unseen into that which is fixed and visible, B ; and said : ' let the strong Arkhas come forth,' and he came forth strong from the invisible, A.   [5] A om.   [6] **Very firm,** B.
[7] **Black,** B.   [8] **The thing,** A ; B OMITS ENTIRE VERSE.   [9] **Bearer** of the created things from all things below, A.   [10] **All,** B.   [11] **Come** forth from below, A Sok.   [12] B om.

God at the creation when he established His throne upon the winds (ὅτε ἀφώριζεν τὸν ἑαυτοῦ θρόνον ἐπ' ἀνέμων).

XXVI. 1. Formation, but not creation, of the earth. **Arkhas** may be from רָקִיעַ or even from ἀρχή.

XXVII. The title is very corrupt.
1. Separation between the light and the darkness: Gen. i. 4. I do

there be a thick substance,' and it was so [1].   2. * And
I spread this out and there was water, and I spread it over
the darkness [2], below the light.   3. And thus I made firm
the waters, that is, the depths, and I surrounded the waters
with light, and I created seven circles and I fashioned them
like crystal, moist and dry, that is to say, like glass and ice,
and as for the waters, and also the other elements, I showed
each of them their paths, (viz.) to the seven stars, each of them
in their heaven, how they should go; and I saw that it was
good.   4. And I separated between the light and the
darkness; that is to say, between the waters here and there.
And I said to the light: ' Let it be day [3]'; and to the darkness, ' Let it be night.' And the evening and the morning
were the first day [4].

XXVIII. 1. [5] And thus I * made firm the circles of the
heavens, and caused the waters * below, which are under the
heavens to be gathered into one place, and that the waves
should be dried up, and it was so.   2. Out of the waves
I made firm and great stones, and out of the stones I heaped
together a dry substance, and I called the dry substance
earth.   3. And in the midst of the earth I appointed
a pit, that is to say an abyss.   4. I gathered the sea into
one place, and I restrained it with a yoke. And I said to

XXVII. [1] And I ordered that they should take from the light and
the darkness and I said: ' Let it be thick and covered with light,' Sok.;
B om.   [2] So A Sok., but that A adds with light after out. B reads And
having clothed (spread out?) certain things with light, I made broad
and stretched out the path of the waters above the darkness.   B
OMITS THE REST OF THE CHAPTER.   [3] Be thou day, Sok.   [4] A adds
as title of XXVIII, Sunday. On it God showed to Enoch all His wisdom
and power: during all the seven days how He created the powers of
the heaven and earth and all moving things and at last man.
XXVIII. [5] A and Sok. agree in this chapter. B is fragmentary and transposed, and reads: (2) And I made the great stones firm, (1) and ordered

---

not pretend to understand what
follows.   3. Seven stars: see
xxx. 5.   4. Gen. i. 4, 5.
    XXVIII. 1. Gen. i. 9.   2.
I called the dry substance earth.

An exact rendering of Gen. i. 10.
3. This may be Sheol, or Tartarus
(cf. xxix. 5), or it may be the abysses
of the waters : cf. Gen. vii. 11 ; viii.
2 ; Eth. En. lxxxix. 7, 8 ; Jubilees ii.

the sea : ' Lo ! I give thee an eternal portion and thou shalt
not move from thy established position.' So I made fast the
firmament and fixed it above the water.   5. This I called
the first day of the creation. Then it was evening, and again
morning, and it was the second day [1].

XXIX. 1. And for all the heavenly hosts I fashioned [2]
a nature like that of fire, and My eye gazed on the very firm
and hard stone. And from the brightness of My eye the
lightning received its wonderful nature.   2. And fire is
in the water and water in the fire, and neither is the one
quenched, nor the other dried up. On this account lightning
is brighter than the sun, and soft water is stronger than hard
stone [3].   3. And from the stone I cut the mighty fire.
*And from the fire I made the ranks of the spiritual hosts,
ten thousand angels [4], *and their weapons are fiery, and

---

the waters of the abysses to dry up, (4) and having collected into rivers
the overflowings of the abysses and the seas into one place, I bound
them with a yoke. I made an everlasting separation between the
earth and the sea, and the waters cannot burst forth. And I made
fast the firmament, and fixed it above the waters.   [1] A adds as title
of the next three verses : The day is Monday, the fiery creations.
    XXIX. [2] B adds the sun of a great light and placed it in the heavens
that it might give light upon earth.   [3] So A and Sok., but that Sok.
adds keener and before brighter. B omits a nature . . . hard stone.
[4] And from stones I created the hosts of spirits, B. A supports text,
but that for ten thousand it read of the ten. B adds and all the starry
hosts, and the Cherubim, and the Seraphim, and the Ophannim, I cut
out of fire.

---

2.   4. Cf. Job xxvi. 10 ; Ps. civ. 9 ;
Prov. viii. 29 ; Jer. v. 22. Firmament : Gen. i. 7, 8. 5. This verse
should be read immediately after xxix,
and together with that chapter should
be restored before xxviii. This is clear
from the analogy of xxx. 1, 2, 7, 8. It
is impossible in its present position.

    XXIX. This chap. is clearly dis-
located from its original position
before xxviii. There is no mark of
time attached to it. The work of the
first day is given in xxv-xxvii ; that

of the second day in xxviii. 1-4 ; that
of the third in xxx. 1. xxviii. 5, as
we have already seen, must have
been differently placed originally.
Hence, if we recall the fact that in
Jubilees ii. 2, and occasionally in
patristic tradition, the creation of the
angels is assigned to the first day—
evidently on the ground of Job
xxxviii. 7.—we can restore the text to
perfect harmony with itself and Jewish
tradition by placing xxix, followed
immediately by xxviii. 5, after xxvii.

their garment is a burning flame, and I ordered them to stand each in their ranks[1].

[Here Satanail was hurled from the Heights with his Angels.]

4. *One of these in the ranks of the Archangels, having turned away with the rank below him, entertained an impossible idea, that he should make his throne higher than the clouds over the earth, and should be equal in rank to My power. 5. And I hurled him from the heights with his angels. And he was flying in the air continually, above the abyss[1].

XXX. 1. *And so I created all the heavens, and it was the

---

[1] B om.

---

3. **From the fire I made the . . . angels.** So Pesikta 3ᴬ : see Weber L. d. J. 161. **4. One of these . . . with the rank below him.** This is clearly Satan. The rank below him is probably the watchers. But however we interpret the text we are beset with difficulties. There are conflicting elements in the text. See xii. and xviii. with notes: vii; xix; xxxi. 3-7 (notes). **Make his throne higher than the clouds.** If this is genuine we must take *clouds* in the sense of heavens. Satan was one of the highest angels before his fall : cf. xviii. 4. Satan and Sammael can not be distinguished in Rabbinic writings. On the attempt of Sammael to found a kingdom see Weber, 244. The following passage from the *Book of Adam and Eve*, I. vi. is evidently derived from our text : 'The wicked Satan . . . set me at naught and sought the Godhead, so that I hurled him down from heaven.' **5. He was flying in the air continu-** ally. This view seems to have been generally received amongst the Jews. Cf. Eph. ii. 2 'The prince of the power of the air'; vi. 12; Test. Benj. 3 τοῦ ἀερίου πνεύματος τοῦ Βελίαρ : Asc. Is. iv. 2 'Berial angelus magnus res huius mundi . . . descendet e firmamento suo'; vii. 9 'Et ascendimus in firmamentum, ego et ille, et ibi vidi Sammaelem eiusque potestates'; x. 29 'descendit in firmamentum ubi princeps huius mundi habitat.' Tuf. haarez, f. 9. 2 'Under the sphere of the moon, which is the last under all, is a firmament . . . and there the souls of the demons are.' Cf. Eisenmenger, ii. 411. According to the Stoics, on the other hand, the abode of the blessed was under the moon. Cf. Tertull. *De An.* 54; Lucan ix. 5 sq. For other authorities see Meyer on Eph. ii. 2; Eisenmenger, ii. 456. It is hard to get a consistent view of the demonology of this book; it seems to be as follows : Satan, one of the archangels (xviii. 4; xxix. 4), seduced the watchers of the

third day.   On the third day [1] I ordered the earth to produce * great trees, such as bear fruit, and mountains [2], and * every sort of herb and every [3] seed that is sown [4], * and I planted Paradise, and enclosed it, and placed fiery angels armed, and so I made a renewing.   2. Then it was evening, and it was morning, being the fourth day [5].   On the fourth day [6] I ordered that there should be great lights in the circles of the heavens.   3. In the first and highest circle I placed the star Kruno; and on the second [7] Aphrodite; on the third

---

XXX. [1] B om. In verse 1 A adds **Tuesday** as title before On the third day. [2] All sorts of trees and high mountains, B. [3] A om. [4] B adds before I produced living things and prepared food for them. [5] B om.; Sok. supports text; but adds of the earth after renewing. A adds **Wednesday** as title of 2[b]–7. [6] B OMITS VERSES 2–7[A]. [7] Sok. adds lower I placed.

---

fifth heaven into revolt, in order to establish a counter kingdom to God, xxix. 4. Therefore Satan, or the Satans (for it is the name of a class) (Weber, 244), were cast down from heaven, xxix. 5 ; xxxi. 4, and given the air for their habitation, xxix. 5. As for his followers, the watchers of the fifth heaven, they were cast down to the second and there kept imprisoned and tortured, vii. 3 ; xviii. 4. Some, however, of the Satans or Watchers went down to earth and married the daughters of men, xviii. 4. From these were born giants, xviii. 5. Thereupon these watchers were imprisoned under the earth, xviii. 6, 7, and the souls of the giants, their children, became subjects of Satan. To return to the Satans, however, when man was created, Satan envied him and wished to make another world, xxxi. 3. Out of envy he tempted Eve to her fall, xxxi. 6.

XXX. 1. Cf. Gen. i. 10, 11. **Mountains.** This is corrupt. We should have a reference here probably to non-fruit-bearing trees, as in Jub. ii. 7 τὰ ξύλα

τὰ κάρπιμά τε καὶ ἄκαρπα. Every seed that is sown. This phrase is found in Jubilees, ii. 7, as one of the third day creations. Paradise. Also in Jub. ii. 7, among the creations of the third day.   2. Circles of the heavens. In Philo, *De Mundi Op.* 38, we find seven circles as here, though with a different meaning: τὸν οὐρανόν φασιν ἑπτὰ διεζῶσθαι κύκλοις. 3. Gen. i. 14–19. In the *Chronography of Joel,* circ. 1200 A. D., p. 34 (ed. Bekker, 1836), the discovery of the signs of the Zodiac, the solstices and the seasons, and the naming of the planets, are assigned to Seth ; but as such discoveries were anciently assigned to Enoch, and were only in later tradition ascribed to Seth, we may not unreasonably regard the mention in Joel of the five planets, Kronos, Zeus, Ares, Aphrodite, Hermes, as ultimately derived from the Enoch literature. The statement in Joel is, ὁ δὲ Σὴθ πρῶτος ἐξεῦρε . . . τὰ σημεῖα τοῦ οὐρανοῦ καὶ τὰς τροπὰς τῶν ἐνιαυτῶν . . . καὶ τοῖς ἄστροις ἐπέθηκεν ὀνόματα καὶ τοῖς πέντε πλανήταις εἰς τὸ

Ares; * on the fourth the Sun [1]; on the fifth Zeus; on the sixth Hermes; on the seventh [2] the moon.   4. And * the lower air I adorned with the lesser stars. 5. And [3] I placed the sun to give light to the day, and the moon and the stars to give light to the night; the sun that he should go * according to each sign of the Zodiac [4]; and the course of * the moon through the twelve signs of the Zodiac [5]. 6. And I fixed their names * and existence, the thunders, and the revolutions of the hours, how they take place [6].   7. Then it was evening and the morning, the fifth day.   * On the fifth day [7] * I commanded the sea to produce [8] fish, * and

---

[1] A om.   [2] A adds the lesser.   [3] And I adorned it with the lesser stars, and on the lower, A.   [4] To every living thing, A.   [5] The twelve months, A.   [6] And their reverberations, and new births, and making of the hours as they go, Sok.   [7] B om. After fifth day A adds Thursday, and after sixth day it adds Friday.   [8] B adds and multiply.

γνωρίζεσθαι ὑπὸ τῶν ἀνθρώπων καὶ μόνον· καὶ τὸν μὲν πρῶτον πλανήτην ἐκάλεσε Κρόνον, τὸν δὲ δεύτερον Δία, τὸν τρίτον Ἄρεα, τὸν τέταρτον Ἀφροδίτην καὶ τὸν πέμπτον Ἑρμῆν. In the mysteries of Mithras, described in Origen, *Contra Celsum* vi. 22, the five planets and the sun and moon are said to be connected by a heavenly ladder. From the first words of the preceding ch. we see that these heavenly bodies had some connexion with the seven heavens, as in our text. The order in which the planets and the sun and moon are mentioned in *Contra Celsum* differs from that given above, and is as follows: Kronos, Aphrodite, Zeus, Hermes, Ares, Selene, Helios. The five planets are first referred to by Philolaus, a Pythagorean, and later by Plato in his *Timaeus*, but not by their individual names (ἥλιός καὶ σελήνη καὶ πέντε ἄλλα ἄστρα ἐπίκλην ἔχοντα πλανῆται). These names, which are not found till we come

down to the *Epinomis*, the work of a disciple of Plato, are enumerated as follows, each with an appellation derived from a god: τὸν τοῦ Κρόνου, τὸν τοῦ Διός, τὸν τοῦ Ἄρεος, τὴν τῆς Ἀφροδίτης, τὸν τοῦ Ἑρμοῦ. According to Archimedes (Macrob. *in Somn. Scip.* i. 19. 2) the order of the planets was as follows: Saturn, Jupiter, Mars, the Sun, Venus, Mercury, the Moon, and this order was generally adopted by Cicero (*de Div.* ii. 43), Manilius (i. 803, 6), Pliny, *H. N.* ii. 6.   The five planets were known to Israel in O. T. times: Kronos as כיון Amos v. 26; Aphrodite as הילל Is. xiv. 12; Ares as נרגל 2 Kings xvii. 30; Zeus as גד Is. lxv. 11; Hermes as נבו Is. xlvi. 1.   5. The Sun . . . according to each sign of the Zodiac. See ch. xiii-xiv. and Eth. En. lxxii. The moon, &c. See lvi. and Eth. En. lxxiii-lxxiv.   7. Cf. Gen. i. 20-26. Observe that most of the creations of the sixth day, Gen.

winged fowls of all kinds [1], and all things that creep upon
the earth, and four-footed things that go about the earth, and
the things that fly in the air, * male and female, and every
living thing breathing with life.   8. And it was evening
and morning the sixth day [1].   * On the sixth day [1] * I ordered
My Wisdom to make man [2] of seven substances.   (1) His
flesh from the earth; (2) his blood * from the dew; (3) his
eyes from the sun [3]; (4) his bones from the stones; (5) his
thoughts from the swiftness of the angels, and the clouds;
(6) his veins [4] and hair from the grass of the earth [5]; (7) his

---

[1] B om.   [2] And when I had finished all I ordered My Wisdom
to make man, B.   B OMITS THE REST OF THE CHAPTER.   [3] From
the dew and the sun (3) his eyes form the abysses of the seas,
Sok.   [4] For veins we should probably read nails. See quotation from
Philo in the Commentary on this verse.   [5] A Sok. add and from the wind
—a manifest dittography.

---

i. 24-26, are here assigned to the
fifth.   8. Ordered my Wisdom. Wisdom is here hypostatized
as in Prov. viii. 30 'Then I was
by him as a master workman.' In
the Book of Wisdom, Wisdom is the
assessor on God's throne, ix. 4; was
with Him when He made the world,
ix. 9; was the instrument by which
all things were created, viii. 5; is the
ruler and renewer of all things, viii.
1; vii. 27. Compare further this
conception of Wisdom with that of the
Logos of Philo, which was the instrument by which God created the world.
Cf. *Leg. All.* iii. 31 σκιὰ θεοῦ δὲ ὁ
λόγος αὐτοῦ ἐστιν, ᾧ καθάπερ ὀργάνῳ
προσχρησάμενος ἐκοσμοποίει : *De
Cherubim* 35 εὑρήσεις γὰρ αἴτιον μὲν
αὐτοῦ τὸν θεόν, ὑφ' οὗ γέγονεν, ὕλην
δὲ τέσσαρα στοιχεῖα, ἐξ ὧν συνεκράθη,
ὄργανον δὲ λόγον θεοῦ, δι' οὗ κατε-
σκευάσθη.   Of seven substances.
The list of these substances is corrupt.
See Critical Notes.   It seems to have
some connexion with the speculations

of the Stoics (G. Sext. *Math.* ix. 81) and
of Philo. Thus, as in our text, man's
body is derived (1) from the earth,
De Mundi Op. 51. Again, whilst in
(4) his bones are derived from stones,
in Philo, *Leg. All.* ii. 7, he is said at
the lowest stage to have a nature in
common with the stones and trees (ἡ
μὲν ἕξις κοινὴ καὶ τῶν ἀψύχων ἐστὶ
λίθων καὶ ξύλων, ἧς μετέχει καὶ τὰ ἐν
ἡμῖν ἐοικότα λίθοις ὀστέα): again
whilst in our text (6) his veins (?)
and hair are from the grass of the
earth, in Philo, *Leg. All.* ii. 7, he is
said in the next higher stage to be
allied to plant-nature, such as the
nails and hair (ἡ δὲ φύσις διατείνει καὶ
ἐπὶ τὰ φυτά· καὶ ἐν ἡμῖν δέ εἰσιν ἐοικότα
φυτοῖς, ὄνυχές τε καὶ τρίχες): finally,
(7) agrees with Philo's doctrine:
cf. *De Mundi Op.* 46. If we could
restore the text as it stood originally
the resemblance would probably be
closer. Philo's view of man's nature
is well summed up in *De Mundi Op.*
51 πᾶς ἄνθρωπος κατὰ μὲν τὴν διάνοιαν

spirit from My spirit and from the wind.   9. And I gave
him seven natures: hearing to his body, sight to his eyes,
smell to the perception, touch to the veins, taste to the blood,
the bones for endurance, sweetness for thought.   10. *I purposed a subtle thing[1]: from the invisible and visible nature
I made man. From both are his death and life, *and his
form[2]; *and the word was like a deed[3] *both small in a
great thing[4], and great in a small thing.   11. And I placed
him upon the earth; like a second angel, in an honourable, great, and glorious way.   12. And I made him a
ruler *to rule upon the earth, and to have My wisdom[5].

---

[1] Lo! I purposed to say a subtle word, Sok.   [2] Sok. om.   [3] A word
is a message as it were something created, Sok.   [4] Both in great
things and in little things, A.   [5] Upon the earth having rule by
My wisdom, Sok.

ᾠκείωται θείῳ λόγῳ, τῆς μακαρίας φύ-
σεως . . . ἀπαύγασμα γεγονώς, κατὰ δὲ
τὴν τοῦ σώματος κατασκευὴν ἅπαντι τῷ
κόσμῳ· συγκέκριται γὰρ ἐκ τῶν αὐτῶν,
γῆς καὶ ὕδατος καὶ ἀέρος καὶ πυρός,
ἑκάστου τῶν στοιχείων εἰσενεγκόντος
τὸ ἐπιβάλλον μέρος πρὸς ἐκπλήρωσιν
αὐταρκεστάτης ὕλης, ἣν ἔδει λαβεῖν
τὸν δημιουργόν, ἵνα τεχνιτεύσηται τὴν
ὁρατὴν ταύτην εἰκόνα. For the later
Talmudic views cf. Weber, 202–204;
Malan's *Book of Adam and Eve*, pp.
209–15. In the Anglo-Saxon Ritual
(circ. 950), to which Dr. Murray has
called my attention, man is said to be
made out of eight substances: 'Octo
pondera de quibus factus est Adam.
Pondus limi, inde factus est caro;
pondus ignis, inde rubeus est sanguis
et calidus; pondus salis, inde sunt
salsae lacrimae; pondus roris, inde
factus est sudor; pondus floris, inde
est varietas oculorum; pondus nubis,
inde est instabilitas mentium; pondus
venti, inde est anhela frigida; pondus
gratiae, inde est sensus hominis.'   9.
Seven natures. Here again the text
is very untrustworthy and the following words seem corrupt: body, veins,
blood, whilst the clauses the bones
. . . thought are quite irrelevant.
Here we should possibly follow Philo,
De Mundi Op. 40 τῆς ἡμετέρας ψυχῆς
τὸ δίχα τοῦ ἡγεμονικοῦ μέρος ἐπταχῆ
σχίζεται, πρὸς πέντε αἰσθήσεις καὶ τὸ
φωνητήριον ὄργανον καὶ ἐπὶ πᾶσι τὸ
γόνιμον, and thus for the corrupt
clauses read the vocal organ and
the generative power. Cp. Test.
Napht. 2.   Philo's division of man's
nature is derived from the Stoics: cf.
Plut. *Plac.* iv. 4 οἱ Στωικοὶ ἐξ ὀκτὼ
μερῶν φασὶ συνιστάναι (τὴν ψυχήν),
πέντε μὲν τῶν αἰσθητικῶν, ὁρατικοῦ,
ἀκουστικοῦ, ὀσφρητικοῦ, γευστικοῦ, ἁπ-
τικοῦ, ἕκτου δὲ φωνητικοῦ, ἑβδόμου
σπερματικοῦ, ὀγδόου αὐτοῦ τοῦ ἡγεμονικοῦ. Cf. also Plut. *Plac.* iv. 21.
10. Man's spiritual and material
nature.   11. Like a second angel.
According to the *Beresh. Rab.* fol.
17, Adam, when first created, reached
from the earth to the firmament. In
the *Book of Adam and Eve*, i. 10,
Adam is called a 'bright angel.'   12.
Gen. i. 26, 28.   13. This verse may

And there was no one like him upon the earth of all My creations.　13. And I gave him a name from the four substances: the East, the West, *the North, and the South[1].　14. And I appointed for him four special stars, and I gave him the name Adam.　15. *And I gave him his will[2], and I showed him the two ways, the light and the

---

[1] A transposes.　　[2] A om.

---

either be the source of or may be derived from the Sibylline Oracles. iii. 24-26

Αὐτὸς δὴ θεός ἐσθ' ὁ πλάσας τετρα-
γράμματον 'Αδάμ,

Τὸν πρῶτον πλασθέντα, καὶ οὔνομα πληρώσαντα

'Αντολίην τε δύσιν τε μεσημβρίην τε καὶ ἄρκτον.

The third line is used frequently, though with a different application, in the Oracles, i. e. ii. 195; viii. 321; xi. 3. It will be observed that this arrangement gives the initials Adma in the wrong order. This etymology is next found in the anonymous writing *De Montibus Sina et Sion*, 4, formerly ascribed to Cyprian: 'Nomen accepit a Deo. Hebreicum Adam in Latino interpretat "terra caro facta," eo quod ex quattuor cardinibus orbis terrarum pugno conprehendit, sicut scriptum est: "palmo mensus sum caelum et pugno conprehendi terram et confinxi hominem ex omni limo terrae; ad imaginem Dei feci illum." Oportuit illum ex his quattuor cardinibus orbis terrae nomen in se portare Adam; invenimus in Scripturis, per singulos cardines orbis terrae esse a conditore mundi quattuor stellas constitutas in singulis cardinibus. Prima stella orientalis dicitur anatole, secunda occidentalis dysis, tertia stella aquilonis arctus, quarta stella meridiana dicitur mesembrion. Ex nominibus stellarum numero quattuor de singulis stellarum nominibus tolle singulas litteras principales, de stella

anatole α, de stella dysis δ, de stella arctos α, de stella mesembrion μ; in his quattuor litteris cardinalibus habes nomen αδαμ.' This etymology is given with approval by Bede, *In Genesim Expositio* iv. 'Hae quattuor literae nominis Adam propria habent nomina in partium nominibus, id est anatole, disis, arctus, mesembria; id est oriens occidens, septentrio, meridies. Et haec proprietas significat dominatu-rum Adam in quattuor supradictis partibus mundi.' It is found also in the *Chronikon* of Glycas (circ. 1150), p. 143: κατὰ τοῦτο δὲ τῷ τοῦ 'Αδάμ ὀνόματι προσηγόρευσεν αὐτὸν . . . καὶ ὅρα τὰ τοῦ τοιούτου ὀνόματος γράμματα· τὰ τέσσαρα γὰρ ὑπεμφαίνουσι κλίματα· ἄλφα ἀνατολή, δέλτα δύσις, ἄλφα ἄρκτος, μῦ μεσημβρία. See Jubilees iii. 28 (notes); Targ.-Jon. on Gen. ii. 7.

14. Four special stars. These stars are named from the four quarters of the earth, and Adam's name is formed from their initial letters. See citation from *De Montibus Sina et Sion*, which seems to be derived from our text. *Stars* may here mean 'angels.' According to the Jalk. Rub. fol. 13; Jalk. Shim. fol. 4 (see *Book of Adam and Eve*, p. 215) certain ministering angels were appointed to wait on Adam. 15. I gave him his will: cf. Tanchuma Pikkude 3 (quoted by Weber, p. 208), ' God does not determine beforehand whether a man shall be righteous or wicked, but puts this in the hands of the man

darkness. And I said unto him : ' This is good and this is
evil ' ; that I should know whether he has love for Me or
hate : that he should appear in his race as loving Me.   16.
I knew his nature, he did not know his nature. Therefore
his ignorance is *a woe to him that he should sin, and

only.' In the text free-will is conceded to man, but this is prejudici-
ally affected by his ignorance (ver.
16): cf. Ecclus. xv. 14, 15 αὐτὸς ἐξ
ἀρχῆς ἐποίησεν ἄνθρωπον καὶ ἀφῆκεν
αὐτὸν ἐν χειρὶ διαβουλίου αὐτοῦ. ἐὰν
θέλῃς συντηρήσεις ἐντολὰς καὶ πίστιν
ποιῆσαι εὐδοκίας. On the question
generally see Joseph. *B. J.* ii. 8. 14;
Antt. xiii. 5. 9; xviii. 1. 3; *Psalms
of Solomon,* ed. by Ryle and James,
pp. 95, 96. 15. The two ways,
the light and the darkness. This
popular figure of the Two Ways was
suggested by Jer. xxi. 8 ' Thus saith
the Lord : Behold, I set before you
the way of life and the way of death ' ;
by Deut. xxx. 15 ' I have set before
thee this day life and good and death
and evil '; Ecclus. xv. 17 ἔναντι ἀνθρώπων ἡ ζωὴ καὶ ὁ θάνατος, καὶ ὃ ἐὰν
εὐδοκήσῃ δοθήσεται αὐτῷ : xvii. 6 καὶ
ἀγαθὰ καὶ κακὰ ὑπέδειξεν αὐτοῖς. For
parallel N. T. expressions cf. Mt. vii.
13, 14; 2 Pet. ii. 2. Of the two
great post-apostolic descriptions of
the Two Ways, in the *Didachè* and
in the *Ep. of Barnabas,* that of the
latter presents the nearest parallel to
our text : chap. xviii. 1 ὁδοὶ δύο εἰσὶν
διδαχῆς καὶ ἐξουσίας, ἥ τε τοῦ φωτὸς
καὶ ἡ τοῦ σκότους. In the *Didachè*
i. 1 we have ὁδοὶ δύο εἰσί, μία τῆς
ζωῆς καὶ μία τοῦ θανάτου: cf. *Test.*
Asher 1 δύο ὁδοὺς ἔδωκεν ὁ θεὸς τοῖς
υἱοῖς ἀνθρώπων . . . ὁδοὶ δύο, καλοῦ καὶ
κακοῦ: Sibyll. Or. viii. 399, 400 αὐτὸς
ὁδοὺς προέθηκα δύο, ζωῆς θανάτου τε
Καὶ γνώμην προέθηκ' ἀγαθὴν ζωὴν
προελέσθαι: cf. also Pastor Hermae

Mand. vi. 1, 2; Clem. Alex. *Strom.*
v. 5; *Apost. Church Order,* iv;
Apost. Constitutions, vii. 1; *Clem.
Homilies* v. 7. I said unto him :
' This is good and this is evil,' &c.
This does not harmonize with the
account in Gen., where the knowledge
of good and evil follows on eating the
forbidden fruit. That I should
know whether he has love for Me
or hate. Deut. xiii. 3 ' Your God
proveth you to know whether ye love
the Lord your God.' 16. Ignorance is a woe to him that he
should sin. This ignorance, as we
see from the preceding verse, is not
first and directly an ignorance of
moral distinctions, but of his nature
with its good and evil impulses
(יצר הטוב and יצר הרע). Ignorance is thus regarded here as an evil
in itself. This is probably the result
of Platonic thought, which had gained
great influence over Hellenistic Judaism, and the idea of the text seems
related, however distantly, to that
ethical system which may be summed
up in the words πᾶς δ' ἄδικος οὐχ ἑκὼν
ἄδικος (Plato, *Legg.* 731 c): οὐδένα
ἀνθρώπων ἑκόντα ἐξαμαρτάνειν (*Prot.*
345 D): κακὸς μὲν γὰρ ἑκὼν οὐδείς
(*Tim.* 86 D). See also *Legg.* 734 B;
Rep. ix. 589 c; *Hipp. Maj.* 296 c.
Herein it is taught that no man wil-
fully chooses evil in preference to
good ; but in every act of moral
judgement the determining motive is
to be found in the real or seeming
preponderance of good in the course
adopted : and that, should this course

I appointed death on account of his sin[1].   17. And[2]
I caused him to sleep, and he slumbered.   And I took from

---

[1] Worse than sinning, and for sin there is nothing else but death,
Sok.   [2] Sok. adds I cast upon him a shadow and.

---

be the worse one, the error of judgement is due either to physical inca-
pacities or faulty education, or to
a combination of both. This view of
sin as an involuntary affection of the
soul follows logically from another
Platonic principle already enunciated by our author (see xxiii. 5, note).
This principle is the pre-existence of
the soul. The soul, as such, according to Platonic teaching, is wholly
good. Evil, therefore, cannot arise
from its voluntary preferences, but
from its limitations, i. e. from its
physical and moral environment,
from its relation to the body and
from wrong education. In the Book
of Wisdom this view is widely di-
verged from. There the body is not
held to be irredeemably evil, but souls
are already good and bad on their
entrance into this life (viii. 19, 20).
In Philo, on the other hand, there is
in the main a return to the Platonic
and Stoic doctrine. The body is
irredeemably evil; it is in fact the
tomb of the soul ($\sigma\hat{\omega}\mu\alpha = \sigma\hat{\eta}\mu\alpha$) ; and
only the sensuously-inclined souls are
incorporated with bodies (see above,
xxiii. 5, note). The views adopted
by our author on these and kindred
points stand in some degree in a closer
relation to the Platonic principles
than do those of Philo or the author
of the Book of Wisdom. Thus he
held : (1) That the soul was created
originally good. (2) That it was not
predetermined either to good or ill
by God, but left to mould its own
destiny (see xxx. 15). (3) That its
incorporation in a body, however,
with its necessary limitations served

to bias its preferences in the direction
of evil. (4) That faithful souls will
hereafter live as blessed incorporeal
spirits, or at all events clothed only
in God's glory (xxii. 7); for there is
no resurrection of the body. Death
on account of his sin. So Ecclus.
xxv. 24 $\dot{\alpha}\pi\dot{\sigma}$ $\gamma\nu\nu\alpha\iota\kappa\dot{\sigma}s$ $\dot{\alpha}\rho\chi\dot{\eta}$ $\dot{\alpha}\mu\alpha\rho\tau\acute{\iota}\alpha s$,
$\kappa\alpha\grave{\iota}$ $\delta\iota'$ $\alpha\dot{\nu}\tau\dot{\eta}\nu$ $\dot{\alpha}\pi o\theta\nu\acute{\eta}\sigma\kappa o\mu\epsilon\nu$ $\pi\acute{\alpha}\nu\tau\epsilon s$;
for 'man was created exactly
like the angels,' Eth. En. lxix. 11,
righteous and immortal, but death
came through sin, Book of Wisdom,
ii. 23, 24; Eth. En. xcviii. 4. The
same teaching is found in the Talmud :
see Weber, 208, 214, 239. This doctrine of man's conditional immortality and of death entering the world
through sin does not belong to O.T.
literature ; for Gen. ii. 17, when
studied in its context, implies nothing
more than a premature death ; for
the law of man's being is enunciated
in Gen. iii. 19 'Dust thou art, and
unto dust shalt thou return,' and his
expulsion from Eden was due first
and principally to the need of guarding against his eating of the tree of
life and living for ever. Furthermore, even in Ecclus., where the idea
of death as brought about by sin is
first enunciated, the doctrine appears
in complete isolation and in open
contradiction to the main statements
and tendencies of the book ; for it
elsewhere teaches that man's mor-
tality is the law from everlasting ($\dot{\eta}$
$\gamma\grave{\alpha}\rho$ $\delta\iota\alpha\theta\acute{\eta}\kappa\eta$ $\dot{\alpha}\pi'$ $\alpha\grave{\iota}\hat{\omega}\nu os$ Ecclus. xiv. 17) :
and that being formed from earth
unto earth must he return, xvii. 1, 2 ;
xl. 11.   Nor again is this doctrine
a controlling principle in the system

him a rib[1], and I made him a wife. ·   18. And by his
wife death came, and I received his last word.   And I called
her by a name, the mother; that is Eve.

[*God gives Paradise to Adam, and gives him Knowledge, so
as to see the Heavens open, and that he should see the
Angels singing a Song of Triumph.*]

XXXI. 1. Adam had a life on earth[2], . . . and I made
a garden in Eden in the East, and (I ordained) that he should
observe the law and keep * the instruction[3].   2. I made
for him the heavens open that he should perceive the angels
singing the song of triumph.   And there was light * without
any[4] darkness continually in Paradise.   3. And the devil
took thought, as if wishing to make another world, because
things were subservient to Adam on earth, to rule it and
have lordship over it.   4. The devil is to be the evil spirit
of the lowest places[5]; * he became Satan, after he left the
heavens.   His name was formerly Satanail[6].   5. And
then, * though he became different from the angels in nature,
he did not change his understanding of just and sinful

---

[1] Sok. adds as he slept.
XXXI. [2] There is evidently a lacuna here.   [3] It, Sok. B OMITS
ENTIRE CHAPTER.   [4] That never knew, Sok.   [5] A adds as he wrought
devilish things.   [6] As flying from the heavens he became Satan,
since his name was Satanail, Sok.

---

of the writers of the Book of Wisdom.
When, however, we come down to
N. T. times we find it the current
view in the Pauline Epistles : cf.
Rom. v. 12 ; I Cor. xv. 21; 2 Cor.
xi. 3. On various views on sin and
death and their causes see Eth. En.
vi–viii ; x. 8; xxxii. 6 ; lxix. 6, 11 ;
xcviii. 4, with notes.   18. By his
wife death came : cf. Ecclus. xxv.
23; 1 Tim. ii. 14. See preceding note.
I received his last word. Corrupt.
XXXI. 2. This verse is almost
quoted in the *Book of Adam and*

Eve I. viii. 'When we dwelt in the
garden . . . we saw the angels that
sang praises in heaven.' According
to S. Ephrem, i. 139, Adam and Eve
lost the angelic vision on their fall
(Malan). Philo, *Quaest.* xxxii. *in
Gen.,* believes 'oculis illos praeditos
esse quibus potuerunt etiam eas quae
in coelo sunt.' For the continual light
in Paradise see *Book of Adam and Eve,*
I. xii ; xiii ; xiv.   3. On the envy
of Satan see Wisdom, ii. 24 ; Joseph.
Antt. i. 1. 4 ; Weber, 211, 244.   4.
See notes on xviii. 3 and xxix. 4.

thoughts[1]. He understood the judgement upon him, and
the former sin which he had sinned.   6. And on account
of this, he conceived designs against Adam; in such a manner
he entered[2] and deceived Eve. But he did not touch Adam.
7. *But I cursed him for (his) ignorance[3]: but those I previously blessed, them I did not curse[4],   8. nor man did
I curse, nor the earth, nor any other things created, but
the evil fruit of man, and then his works.

[*On account of the Sin of Adam, God sends him to the Earth,
'From which I took thee,' but He does not wish to destroy
him in the Life to come.*]

XXXII. 1. I said to him: 'Earth thou art, and to earth
also from whence I took thee shalt thou return. I will not
destroy thee, but will send thee whence I took thee. Then
I can also take thee in My second coming'; and I have
blessed all My creation, visible and invisible[5].   2. And
I blessed the seventh day, * which is the Sabbath[6], for in it
I rested from all My labours.

[*God shows Enoch the Duration of this World, 7000 Years, and
the eighth Thousand is the End. (There will be) no Years,
no Months, no Weeks, no Days.*]

XXXIII. 1. Then also I established the eighth day. Let

---

[1] Though he was changed from the angels, he did not change his
nature, but he had thought, as is the mind of just men and sinners, Sok.
[2] Sok. adds into Paradise.   [3] Sok. om.   [4] Sok. adds and those whom
before I had not blessed, them also I did not curse.
XXXII. [5] A adds (against B Sok.) And Adam was five and a half hours
in Paradise. B OMITS ENTIRE CHAPTER.   [6] Sok. om.

6. See xxx. 18, note; Weber, 211, 244.
7. Cursed him for (his) ignorance.
This ought to refer to the Serpent or
to Satan.

XXXII. 1. My second coming.
God's coming to judge the earth, to
bless His people, and to punish their
enemies. This is called καιρὸς ἐπισκοπῆς

and ἡμέρα διαγνώσεως in the Book
of Wisdom, iii. 7, 18. It is referred
to again in xlii. 5 of our text. God's
first coming to the earth was for the
sake of Adam and to bless all that He
had made, lviii. 1.

XXXIII. 1, 2. From the fact that
Adam did not live to be 1000 years

the eighth be the first * after My work [1], and let * the days [2]
be after the fashion of seven thousand.   2. * Let there be
at the beginning of the eighth thousand a time when there
is no computation, and no end; neither years, nor months,
nor weeks, nor days, nor hours [3].   3. And now Enoch, what

XXXIII. [1] Of my rest, Sok. B OMITS VERSES 1, 2.   [2] A om.   [3] And
let the eighth day be for a beginning in the likeness of eight thousand.
So concerning the first day of My rest, and also the eighth day of My
rest, let them return continually, Sok. Margin of Sok.'s MS. reads : the
beginning of unrighteousness, the time without end, neither years, nor
months, nor weeks, nor days, nor hours.

---

old, the author of the Book of Jubilees,
iv. 30, concludes that the words of
Gen. ii. 17 'In the day thou eatest
thereof thou shalt surely die' were
actually fulfilled. It is hence obvious
that already before the Christian era
1000 years had come to be regarded
as one world-day. To arrive at the
conception of a world-week of 7000
years—6000 years from the creation
to the judgement, followed by 1000
years, or a millennium of blessedness
and rest—it was necessary to proceed
but one step further, and this step
we find was taken by the author of
our text. In Irenaeus, moreover,
Contra Haer. v. 28. 3 this reasoning is
given explicitly : ὅσαις . . . ἡμέραις
ἐγένετο ὁ κόσμος, τοσαύταις χιλιοντάσι
συντελεῖται. Καὶ διὰ τοῦτό φησιν ἡ
γραφή. Καὶ συνετέλεσεν ὁ θεὸς τῇ
ἡμέρᾳ ς΄ τὰ ἔργα αὐτοῦ ἃ ἐποίησε, καὶ
κατέπαυσεν ἐν τῇ ἡμέρᾳ τῇ ζ΄ ἀπὸ
πάντων τῶν ἔργων αὐτοῦ. τοῦτο δ᾽ ἐστὶ
τῶν προγεγονότων διήγησις καὶ τῶν ἐσο-
μένων προφητεία· ἡ γὰρ ἡμέρα κυρίου ὡς
ͺα ἔτη. ἐν ἓξ οὖν ἡμέραις συντετέλεσται τὰ
γεγονότα. φανερὸν οὖν ὅτι ἡ συντέλεια
αὐτῶν τὸ ͵ς ἔτος ἐστί. Clemens Alex.
Strom. iv. 25 refers to this conception—
possibly to our text. It is not improbable that the statements of Cedrenus
on this head are drawn from our text.
Thus on p. 9 he writes : τούτου χάριν

ηὐλογήθη καὶ αὕτη (ἡ ἡμέρα) ὑπὸ τοῦ
θεοῦ καὶ ἡγιάσθη καὶ σάββατον ὡς κατα-
παύσιμος προσηγορεύθη, καὶ ὡς τύπος
τῆς ἑβδόμης χιλιοετηρίδος καὶ τῶν
ἁμαρτωλῶν συντελείας, ὡς Ἰώσηππος
μαρτυρεῖ καὶ ἡ λεπτὴ Γένεσις ἣν καὶ
Μωσέως εἶναί φασί τινες ἀποκάλυψιν.
It is, we repeat, not improbable that
our text is the original source of
Cedrenus' statements, inasmuch as
nothing of the kind is found either in
Josephus or the Book of Jubilees,
from which he professes to derive
them. Syncellus, on whom Cedrenus
is largely dependent, is frequently
wrong in his references in the case of
Apocalyptic literature. A most interesting expansion and an adaptation of the text to Christian conceptions are to be found in Augustin,
De Civ. xxii. 30. 5 'Ipse etiam
numerus aetatum, veluti dierum, si
secundum eos articulos temporis com-
putetur qui in Scripturis videntur
expressi, iste Sabbatismus evidentius
apparebit, quoniam septimus inveni-
tur : ut prima aetas, tanquam dies
primus sit ab Adam usque ad dilu-
vium, secunda inde usque ad Abraham . . . ab Abraham usque ad David
una, altera inde usque ad transmi-
grationem in Babyloniam, tertia inde
usque ad Christi carnalem nativitatem.
Fiunt itaque omnes quinque. Sexta

things I have told thee, * and what thou hast understood, and
what heavenly things thou hast seen [1], and what thou hast
seen upon the earth, and what * thou hast [2] written in books,
by My wisdom all these things I devised * so as to create
them [3], and I made them from the highest foundation to the
lowest, * and to the end [1].　　4. And there is no counsellor [4]
* nor inheritor of My works [1]. I am the eternal One, and the
One not made with hands : * My thought is without change,
My wisdom is My counsellor [5] and My word is reality ; and
My eyes see all things, * if I look to all things [3] they * stand
fast [6]. If I turn away My face, all are in need of Me.　　5.
And now pay attention, Enoch, and know thou who is
speaking to thee, and do thou take the books which thou
thyself hast written.　　6. And I give thee * Samuil and
Raguil [7] who brought thee * to Me [3]. And go * with them [8]
upon the earth, and tell thy sons what things I have said to

---

[1] B om.　[2] I have, A.　[3] A om.　[4] Lamp, B.　[5] My thought
is a lamp, B.　[6] Stand and tremble with fear, A Sok.　[7] Semil and
Rasuil, B ; B adds and him.　[8] B Sok. om.

---

nunc agitur . . . post hanc tanquam
in die septimo requiescet Deus, cum
eundem septimum diem, quod nos
erimus, in se ipso Deo faciet requies-
cere. . . . Haec tamen septima erit
Sabbatum nostrum, cuius finis non
erit vespera, sed dominicus dies velut
octavus aeternus. . . . Ecce quod erit
in fine sine fine.' For other speculations in reference to the world-week
see *Evang. Nicodemi,* ii. 12 ; *Book
of Adam and Eve,* I. iii. A time
when there is no computation . . .
neither years nor months, &c.
Sibyll. Or. viii. 424–427 may have
been influenced by our text where it
speaks of the eternity of blessedness :

Ούκ έτι λοιπόν έρεις λυπούμενος·'' αΰ-
ριον έσται,''

Ούκ '' έχθὲς γέγονεν '' ούκ ήματα πολλὰ μερίμνης,

Ούκ έαρ, ού χειμών, ούτ' άρ θέρος, ού
μετόπωρον,

Ού δύσις άντολίη·' ποιήσω γαρ μακρὸν
ήμαρ.

3. I made them from the highest
foundation to the lowest : cf.
Ecclus. xviii. 1 ὁ ζῶν εἰς τὸν αἰῶνα
έκτισε τὰ πάντα κοινῇ, where κοινῇ is
a rendering of יחד. 4. My
thought is without change. Num.
xxiii. 19 ; 1 Sam. xv. 29 ; Ezek. xxiv.
14. My wisdom is My coun-
sellor. See xxx. 8 (note). Cf.
Ecclus. xlii. 22 καὶ ού προσεδεήθη
ούδενὸς συμβούλου. My word is
reality. So Eth. En. xiv. 22 (Gk.)
πᾶς λόγος αύτοῦ έργον. Cf. Ps. xxxiii.
9 ; Ecclus. xlii. 15 ἐν λόγοις κυρίου τὰ
έργα αύτοῦ. My eyes see all things :
cf. Ecclus. xxxix. 19. If I turn
away My face, &c. Ps. civ. 29
' Thou hidest Thy face, they are

thee, and what thou hast seen from the lowest heaven up to
My throne.   7. For I have created all the hosts, and all the
powers, and there is none that opposes Me, or is disobedient
to Me.   For all are obedient to My sole power, and labour for
My rule alone.   8. Give [1] them the works written out by
thee, *and they shall read them, and know Me to be the
Creator of all; and shall understand that there is no other
God beside Me [2].   9. *They shall distribute the books of
thy writing to their children's children [3], and from generation
to generation, and from nation to nation.   10. *And I will
give thee, Enoch, My messenger, the great captain Michael,
for thy writings and for the writings of thy fathers, Adam,
Seth, Enos, Kainan, Malaleel, and Jared, thy father [4].   11.
*And I shall not require them till the last age, for I have
instructed My two angels, Ariukh and Pariukh, whom I have
put upon the earth as their guardians.   12. And I have ordered
them in time to guard them that the account of what I shall
do in thy family may not be lost in the deluge to come [5].

---

[1] I will give, A.   [2] B om.   [3] Let the children give them to
the children, B.   [4] As being the messenger Enoch of my captain
Michael. Because that thy writings and the writings of thy fathers,
Adam and Sit, B.   [5] (Because these) will not be required till
the last age, I have ordered my angels, Oriokh and Mariokh, to give
orders to guard in season the writings which I have placed upon
the earth, and that they should guard the writings of thy fathers, so
that what I have wrought in thy family may not be lost, B; A om. In
the text I have followed Sok., but that for to punish them I have read to
guard them with B.

---

troubled.'   6. Cf. Eth. En. lxxxi.
5, 6. Samuil. This is either from
שְׁמוּעַ אֵל = heard of God, 1 Sam. i.
20, or from שָׁמוּ and אֵל = name of
God. Raguil is a transliteration of
רְעוּאֵל = friend of God.   9. Cf.
xlvii. 2, 3; xlviii. 7-9; liv; lxv. 5;
Eth. En. lxxxii. 1, 2, where, exactly
as here, the books are to be trans-
mitted straightway to the generations
of the world, whereas in i. 2; xciii.
10; civ. 12 the method and times
of the disclosure of the books are
different. Though the writings are

committed to the keeping of men,
they are under the guardianship of
special angels until the time for their
complete disclosure and understanding has come. See verses 11, 12.
10. Michael was the guardian angel
of Israel: Dan. x. 13, 21; xii. 1.
See Eth. En. ix. 1; x. 11; xx. 5
(note); xl. 4, &c.; Weber, 165.   11.
Till the last age. At last the time
for the due comprehension of these
books will arrive: see ver. 9, note;
xxxv. 2, 3; (liv); Eth. En. xciii.
10; civ. 12. Ariukh. This proper

[*God accuses the Idolators ; the Workers of Iniquity, such as Sodom, and on this account He brings the Deluge upon them.*]

XXXIV. 1. *For I know the wickedness of men that they will not bear the yoke which I have put upon them, nor sow the seeds which I have given them, but will cast off My yoke and accept another, and sow vain seeds and bow to vain gods, and deny Me the only God[1].   2. And they will fill all the world with *wickedness and iniquity, and foul impurities with one another, sodomy and all other impure practices, which it is foul to speak about[2].   3. And on this account I will bring a deluge upon the earth *and I will destroy all[3], and[4] the earth shall be destroyed in great corruption.

[*God leaves one Just Man from the Family of Enoch, with all his House, which pleased God according to His Will.*]

XXXV. 1. And I will leave a righteous man *of thy race[5], with all his house who shall act according to My will.   From

---

XXXIV. [1] Sok. supports text but that it omits nor sow ... given them. A reads: They turned from My law and My yoke and raised up worthless races such as feared not God nor worshipped Me, but began to bow before vain gods, and denied Me, the only God.   [2] Unjust deeds and harlotries and services of idols, B; Sok. adds and evil service.   [3] B Sok. omit.   [4] A adds all.
XXXV. [5] A B om.

---

name is found in Gen. xiv. 1, 9; Dan. ii. 14. The derivation is doubtful, being êri-aku = servant of the moon-god (Delitzsch), or a compound from אֲרִי : hence a lionlike man (Gesenius).

XXXIV. 1. Cast off My yoke : cf. for phrase xlviii. 9; Ecclus. xxviii. 19, 20; Matt. xi. 29. **Sow vain seeds.** This is obscure. The words seem to be metaphorical and not to refer to Deut. xxii. 9. **Deny, &c. :** cf. Josh. xxiv. 27.   **2.** It is this verse that is referred to. in Test. Napht. 4, though it is there somewhat

differently applied : ἀνέγνων ἐν γραφῇ ἁγίᾳ Ἐνώχ, ὅτι καίγε καὶ ὑμεῖς ἀποστήσεσθε ἀπὸ κυρίου, πορευόμενοι κατὰ πᾶσαν πονηρίαν ἐθνῶν, καὶ ποιήσετε κατὰ πᾶσαν ἀνομίαν Σοδόμων.   **3.** The words immediately subsequent to those just quoted from Test. Napht. seem to be in part derived from this verse : καὶ ἐπάξει ὑμῖν κύριος αἰχμαλωσίαν . . . ἕως ἂν ἀναλώσῃ κύριος πάντας ὑμᾶς is simply an adaptation of I will bring a deluge upon the earth, and I will destroy all.

XXXV. 1. Righteous man, i. e.

E

their seed * after some time [1] will be raised up a numerous [2] generation, but * of these, many will be [1] very insatiable. 2. Then on the extinction of that family, I will show them the books of thy writings, and of thy fathers, and the guardians of them on earth will show them to the men who are true, * and please Me, who do not take My name in vain [1].   3. And they shall tell to another [3] generation, and these * having read them [1], shall be glorified at last more than before.

[*God ordered Enoch to live on the Earth thirty Days, so as to teach his Sons, and his Sons' Sons. After thirty Days he was thus taken up into Heaven.*]

XXXVI. 1. And now, Enoch, I give thee a period [4] of thirty days to work in thy house. And tell thou thy sons [5], * and all thy household before Me; that they may listen to what is spoken to them by thee [6]; that they read and understand, how there is no other God beside Me ; * and let them always keep My commandments, and begin to read and understand the books written out by thee [6].   2. And after thirty days, I will send My angels [7] for thee, and they [8] shall take thee from the earth, and from thy sons, * according to My will [9].

[*Here God summons an Angel.*]

[XXXVII. 1. And God called one of His greatest angels,

---

[1] B om.   [2] Another, Sok.   [3] That, B.
XXXVI. [4] Sok. adds of preparation.   [5] B adds all that thou guardest in thy heart.   [6] B om.   [7] Angel, A Sok.   [8] He, A Sok.   [9] To Me, A Sok.

Noah. 2. On the extinction of that family. This seems to refer to the destruction of the wicked during the period of the sword. About the same time the books of Enoch were to be given to the righteous. See for the same connexion of ideas Eth. En. xciii. 9, 10; xci. 12. The guardians. See xxxiii. 9, 11 (notes).   3. The period of the sword and the disclosure of Enoch's books introduces the Messianic age.

XXXVI. 1. In Eth. En. lxxxi. 6 the period is one year. Read and understand, &c.: cf. Eth. En. lxxxii. 1–3.   2. Cf. Eth. En. lxxxi. 6.

XXXVII. This chapter, which

*terrible and awful [1], and placed him by me, *and the appearance of that angel was like [2] snow, and his hands were like ice ; * he had a very cold appearance [3], and my face was chilled because I could not endure * the fear of the Lord [4] ; *just as it is not possible to [5] endure the mighty fire and heat of the sun, and the frost of the air.   2. And the Lord said to me, ' Enoch, if thy face is not chill here; no man can look upon thy face [6].']

[*Mathusal had Hope, and awaited his Father Enoch by his Bed, Day and Night.*]

XXXVIII. 1 [7]. And the Lord said to those men who first took me : ' Take Enoch with you to the earth, and wait for him till the appointed day.'   2. And at night they placed me upon my bed, and Mathusal, expecting my coming by day and by night, was a guard at my bed.   3. And he was terrified when he heard my coming, and I gave him directions that all my household should come, that I might tell them everything.

[*The mournful Admonition of Enoch to his Sons, with Weeping and great Sorrow, speaking to them [8].*]

XXXIX. 1. *Listen, my children, what things are according to the will of the Lord. I am sent to-day to you to tell you from the lips of the Lord, what was and what is happening now, and what will be before the day of

---

XXXVII. [1] In a voice like thunder, B.   [2] In appearance he was white as, A.   [3] In appearance having great cold, Sok. ; B om.   [4] The great terror and awe, B.   [5] For I could not, A ; B omits just as . . . frost of the air.   [6] B om.
XXXVIII. [7] B OMITS ENTIRE CHAPTER.
XXXIX. [8] The Instructions given by Enoch to his Sons, B.

---

is found in all the MSS., is read in its present position in A Sok., but after xxxix in B. I have bracketed it as
it seems irrelevant to the entire text.   **XXXVIII.** 1. Cf. xxxvi.   2. Cf. i. 2-4.   3. Cf. Eth. En. xci. 1.

judgement.   2. Hear, my children, for I do not speak
to you to-day from my lips, but from the lips of the Lord
who has sent me to you.   For you hear [1] * the words of my
lips, a mortal man like yourselves [2].   3. * I have seen the
face of the Lord as it were iron that is heated in the fire, and
when brought out sends forth sparks and burns.   4. Look
at the eyes of me [3], * a man laden with a sign for you [4].
* I have seen the eyes of the Lord shining like a ray of the
sun and striking with terror human eyes.   5. You, my
children, see the right hand of a man [3] * made like yourselves [5]
* assisting you.   I have seen the right hand of the Lord
assisting me, and filling the heavens.   6. You see the
* compass of my actions, like to your own [6].   I have seen the
measureless and harmonious [7] form of the Lord.   To Him
there is no end.   7. You therefore hear the words of my
lips, but I have heard the words of the Lord, like great
thunder, with continual agitation of the clouds.   8. And
now, * my children [3], listen to the [8] discourses * of your earthly
father [3].   It is terrible and awful to stand before the face
of an earthly prince—* terrible and very awful [3] because
the will of the prince is death and the will of the prince
is life [9]; how much more is it terrible and awful to stand
before the face of the * Lord of lords, and of the earthly [10] and
the heavenly hosts.   Who can endure this never-ending
terror ?

----

[1] 1. Hear, my children, my beloved ones, the admonition of your
father: how according to the will of God, I am sent to you now.
What exists and what was, and what is happening now, and what will
be before the day of judgement, I do not now tell you from my own lips,
but from the lips of the Lord; for the Lord sent me to you.   2. And
do you therefore hear, A.   I was sent of late to tell you from the lips
of the Lord what things are, and what shall be before the day of judgement. And now, my children, I do not speak to you from my own lips,
but from the lips of the Lord, B.   [2] B om.; Sok. adds I have heard from
the fiery lips of the Lord : for the lips of the Lord are like a fiery
furnace, and his angels [winds] are a flame of fire going forth.   You,
my children, as that of a man made like yourselves, but.   [3] B om.
[4] A man in his marks just like you, Sok. ; B om.   [5] A B om.   [6] So
A Sok., but that for actions Sok. reads body ; B om.   [7] Incomparable, B.
B transposes 6 [b] after 7.   [8] My, B.   [9] A om.; B adds or great terrors,
and omits the rest of the verse.   [10] Heavenly Ruler, the Lord of the
living and the dead, A.

[*Enoch instructs faithfully his Children about all Things from the Mouth of the Lord; how he saw, and heard and wrote them down.*]

XL. 1. And now, my children, I know all things [1] from the lips of the Lord; for [2] my eyes have seen from the beginning to the end [3].   2. I know all things and have written all things in the books, both the heavens and the end of them, and their fulness, and all the hosts, and I have measured their goings, and written down the stars and their innumerable quantity. 3. What man has seen their alternations and their goings? Not even the angels know their number; I have written down the names of all.   4. And I have measured the circle of the sun, and I have measured his rays; * and his coming in and going out, through all the months, and all his courses, and their names I have written down.   5. I have measured the circle of the moon, and its waning which occurs during every day, and the secret places in which it hides every day and ascends according to all the hours.   6. I have laid down the four seasons, and from the seasons I made four circles, and in the circles I placed the years; I placed the months, and from the

---

XL. [1] A Sok. add **One thing I have learned.** Throughout this chapter B is transposed in every way imaginable. B OMITS VERSES 2–7.   [2] And another, A Sok.   [3] Sok. adds **and from the end to the return.**

XL. 1. **I know all things ... my eyes have seen,** &c. This seems to be the passage to which Clem. Alex. *Eclog. Proph.* (Dind. iii. 456) refers: ὁ Δανιὴλ λέγει ὁμοδοξῶν τῷ Ἐνὼχ τῷ εἰρηκότι 'καὶ εἶδον τὰς ὕλας πάσας': and Origen (*de Princ.* iv. 35) 'scriptum namque est in eodem libello dicente Enoch universas materias perspexi.' Cf. Sibyll. Or. viii. 375, where, in a passage recalling several phrases of this chapter, ἀρχὴν καὶ τέλος οἶδα, ὃς οὐρανὸν ἔκτισα καὶ γῆν.   2. **Stars and their innumerable quantity.**

Cf. Eth. En. xliii. 1, 2; xciii. 14. 3. **Not even the Angels,** &c. Cf. xxiv. 3. 4. See xiii, xiv (notes). 5. See xvi (notes). **Its waning which,** &c. There is not a single reference to this phenomenon in the Slav. Enoch, but there is a complete account of its waxing and waning in Eth. En. lxxiv. **Secret places in which it hides,** &c. Corrupt. 6. **I have laid down the four seasons.** In xiii. 5 we have a reference to the four seasons, but in Eth. En. lxxxii. 11–20 there is an account which, though

months I calculated the days, and from the days [1] I have
*calculated [2] the hours [3].   7. Moreover, I have written
down all things *moving [4] upon the earth [5].   *I have
written down all things that are nourished [6], all seed sown
and unsown, which grows on the earth, and all things
belonging to the garden, and every herb and every flower,
and their fragrance and their names.   8. And the dwellings
of the clouds, *and their conformations and their wings [7],
how they bring rain and *the rain-drops, I investigated all.
9. And I-wrote down the course of the [7] thunder *and
lightning [7], and they [8] showed me the keys, *and their
guardians [9] and their path [10] by which they go.   They are
brought forth in bonds, in measured degree, *and are let go
in bonds [1], lest by their *heavy course and vehemence [11] they
should overload the clouds of wrath and destroy everything
on earth.   10. I have written down the treasuries of the
snow, and the store-houses of the hail, and the cool breezes.
*And I observed the holder of the keys of them during the
season: and how he fills the clouds with them [12], and yet
does not exhaust their treasuries.   11. I *wrote down [13]
the abodes of the winds, *and I observed and saw [7] how those
who hold *their keys [14] bear balances and measures, and in
the first place they put them on a balance, in the second they [15]
let them go in measure *moderately, with care [7] over the
whole earth, so that with their heavy breathing they should

---

[1] A om.   [2] **Measured and calculated, Sok.**   [3] Sok. adds and written
them down.   [4] That were arranged, Sok.   [5] Sok. adds making
inquiries into them.   [6] Sok. om.   [7] B om.   [8] The angels, B.
[9] Which guarded them, B.   [10] Coming in and going out, Sok.
[11] Grievous vehemence, B. Heavy opening (?) and vehemence, Sok.
[12] I saw at that time how the clouds are restrained by them as a key
does prisoners, B. I watched their seasons: how those that hold the
keys of them fill the clouds with them, Sok.   [13] Saw, B.   [14] Keys
of their prisons, B.   [15] B adds measure and.

---

now defective, was clearly complete
originally. 8. Cf. Eth. En. lx. 19–
22 for an account of these phenomena.
9. Course of the thunder, &c.

This is to be found in Eth. En. lix;
lx. 13-15.   10. Cf. vi. 1, 2; Eth.
En. lx. 17, 18.   11. See Eth. En.
xli. 4.

not shake the whole [1] earth.   12. * For I have measured the whole earth, its mountains and all hills, fields, trees, stones, rivers; all things that exist I have written down, the height from earth to the seventh heaven, and down to the lowest hell[1], * the place of judgement and the mighty hell[2] laid open, and * full of lamentation. And I saw how [1] the prisoners suffer, awaiting the immeasurable judgement.   13. * And I wrote out all of those who are being judged by the judge, and all the judgement they receive, and all their deeds [1].

---

[1] B om.   [2] From thence I was taken to the place of judgement, and I saw hell, B.   I append here chapter XL in full, as it appears in B. This chapter in B is manifestly fragmentary and disarranged, and serves to justify the originality of the fuller form as preserved in A Sok. 1. My children, I know all from the lips of the Lord. For mine eyes saw from the beginning to the end, 8. and the dwelling places of the clouds, 9. with those which bring storms and thunder. And the angels showed me the keys which guarded them. 10. I saw the treasure of snow and ice, 9. and the path by which they go: they are brought forth in bonds in measure, and let go in bonds, so that with grievous vehemence they should not oppress the clouds and destroy in the earth, 10. both the air and the cold. I saw at that time how the clouds are restrained by them as a key does prisoners, and they are not allowed to exhaust their treasuries. 11. I saw the abodes of the winds, how those who hold the keys of their prisons bear with them the balances and the measures : in the first place they lay on the balances; in the second they measure, and in measure do they let them go over the whole earth : so that by their powerful breath they should not shake the earth. 12. From thence I was taken to the place of judgement and I saw hell open and the prisoners and the eternal judgement.

---

12. Down to the lowest hell. We come here upon a conception irreconcilable with the general scheme of the author. Hell, according to this scheme, is really located in the third heaven. See x, where the place, its horrors, and the classes it is prepared for, are described at length. But the old Jewish beliefs of an underworld of punishment are too strong to be wholly excluded, and so consistency is here sacrificed to completeness. For an analogous comparison cf. xviii. 7. It is possible, further, that the author may have had some idea of a series of seven hells, as he speaks here of 'the lowest hell,' and as this idea is afterwards found in Rabbinic tradition; see Eisenmenger, ii. 302, 328-330. If, however, we observe how close this hell is to the Garden of Eden, in xlii. 3, we shall be inclined to identify it with the place of punishment described in x. The interpretation, however, of xlii. 3 is difficult. Awaiting the immeasurable judgement. These words, which are found also in vii. 1, in reference to the fallen watchers, would seem to imply an intermediate place of punishment, in fact, Sheol or Hades. 13. This was an ancient belief of the Jews : cf. liii. 2 ; lxiv. 5 ; Jubilees iv. 23 ; x. 17.

[How Enoch wept for the Sins of Adam.]

XLI. 1. And I saw * all our forefathers from the beginning with Adam and Eve [1], and I sighed and wept, * and spake of the ruin (caused by) their wickedness [2] : * Woe is me for my infirmity and that of my forefathers [1].　2. And * I meditated in my heart and said [3] : 'Blessed is the man who was not born, or, having been born, has never sinned before the face of the Lord, so that he should not come into this place, to bear the yoke of this place!'

[How Enoch saw those who keep the Keys, and the Guardians of the Gates of Hades standing by.]

XLII. 1. I saw * those who keep the keys, and are the guardians of the gates of hell, standing [4], like great serpents,

---

XLI. [1] B om.　[2] The destruction of the unholy, B.　[3] I said in my heart, B.

XLII. [4] The guardians of hell holding the keys, standing opposite to the gates, B. B blends xli and xlii. 1–2 together in this order, xlii. 1 ; xli ; xlii. 2. It will be seen that it omits reference to Adam and Eve.

From being the scribe of God's works, as he is universally in the Eth. and the Slav. Enoch, the transition was easy to the conception of Enoch as a scribe of the deeds of men. Cf. for later tradition Test. Abraham (ed. James), p. 115 καὶ εἶπεν Ἀβραὰμ πρὸς Μιχαήλ· Κύριε, . . . τίς ἐστιν ὁ ἄλλος ὁ ἐλέγχων τὰς ἁμαρτίας ; καὶ λέγει Μιχαὴλ πρὸς Ἀβραάμ . . . ὁ ἀποδεικνύμενος οὗτός ἐστιν ὁ διδάσκαλυς τοῦ οὐρανοῦ καὶ τῆς γῆς καὶ γραμματεὺς τῆς δικαιοσύνης Ἐνώχ· ἀπέστειλεν γὰρ κύριος αὐτοὺς ἐνταῦθα, ἵνα ἀπογράφωσιν τὰς ἁμαρτίας καὶ τὰς δικαιοσύνας ἑκάστου.

XLI. 1. It seems to be implied here that the forefathers of Enoch, including Adam and Eve, are in the place of punishment, and that they are to remain there till God comes to judge the world (xlii. 5, note). That

Adam and the patriarchs were in Hades was a prevalent early Christian belief. Cf. *Descensus ad Inferos*, viii–ix. 2. Cf. 4 Ezra iv. 12 'Melius erat nos non adesse quam advenientes . . . pati.' Eth. En. xxxviii. 2; Apoc. Bar. x. 6.

XLII. 1. Who keep the keys. In Sibyll. Or. viii. 121–2 we have a strange application of this idea :

　　αἰὼν κοινὸς ἅπασιν κλειδοφύλαξ εἱρκτῆς μεγάλης ἐπὶ βῆμα θεοῖο.

Keys. Cf. Rev. ix. 1 ; xx. 1. Guardians of the gates of hell. According to Emek hammelech, fol. 144, col. 2, each division of hell is under the control of a certain angel (Eisenmenger, ii. 332). The Greek word here may have been τημελοῦχοι. In the singular number it has become a proper name in Apoc. Pauli. Like

and their faces were like quenched lamps, and their eyes were fiery [1], and their teeth were sharp [2].   * And they were stripped to the waist [3].   2. And I said * before their faces [4], 'Would that I had not seen you, * nor heard of your doings [5], * and that those of my race had never come to you [6] ! * Now they have only sinned a little in this life, and always suffer in the eternal life [7].'   3. * I went out to the East, to the paradise of Eden, where rest has been prepared for the just, and it is open to the third heaven, and shut from this world [8]. 4. * And guards are placed at the very great gates of the east of the sun, i. e. fiery angels, singing triumphant songs, that never cease rejoicing in the presence of the just. 5. At the last coming they will lead forth Adam with our forefathers, and conduct them there, that they may rejoice, as a man calls those whom he loves to feast with him ; and they having come with joy hold converse, before the dwelling of that man [7], * with joy awaiting his feast, the enjoyment and the immeasurable wealth, and joy and merriment in the light, and eternal life [9].   6. * Then

---

[1] Like a darkened flame, B.   [2] B Sok. om.   [3] A om.   [4] To the persons (there), B.   [5] B om. A OMITS VERSES 2-14ᵃ.   [6] Nor brought my family to you, Sok.   [7] B om.   [8] B seems to recall this verse in the words : And I saw there a blessed place and every created thing blessed. B introduces this section with the words : Entry of Enoch unto the Paradise of the Just.   [9] And all living there in joy and in boundless happiness and eternal life, B.

quenched lamps. Contrast the faces and eyes of the heavenly angels, i. 5. 2. Cf. xli. 2. 3. The expression 'open to the third heaven' is strange ; it would seem to imply that this is not the heavenly Paradise in the third heaven, but the original Garden of Eden. On the other hand, as this Paradise is prepared for the righteous, we are obliged to identify it with the Paradise of this third heaven described in viii-ix.   5. The last coming. See xxxii. 1 (note) ; lviii. 1. Adam with our forefathers. See

xli. 1 (note). The idea that the patriarchs were in hell or hades is at variance with what is stated or implied in some parts of the Eth. En. Cf. lx. 8, 23 ; lxi. 12 ; lxx. 3, 4, where we find Paradise already peopled with the righteous ; but it is not incompatible with lxxxix. 52 ; xciii. 8, where apparently Enoch and Elijah are its only inhabitants. According to xxii the patriarchs were to remain in hades till the final judgement. This would, in some degree, harmonize with our text.   6-14. Nine

I said [1], 'I tell you, my children: blessed is he who fears
* the name of the Lord. and serves continually before His
face, and brings his gifts with fear continually in this life [2],
* and lives all his life justly, and dies [3].   7. Blessed is he
who executes a just judgement, * not for the sake of recompense, but for the sake of righteousness, expecting nothing
in return : a sincere judgement shall afterwards come to
him [3].   8. * Blessed is he who clothes the naked with
a garment, and gives his bread to the hungry.   9. Blessed
is he who gives a just judgement for the orphan and
the widow, and assists every one who is wronged [4].
10. Blessed is he who turns from the * unstable path of this
vain world [5], and walks by the righteous path * which leads
to eternal life [3].   11. Blessed is he who sows just seed,

---

[1] Sok. om.   [2] And serves the Lord; and do you, my children,
learn to bring gifts to the Lord that you may have life, B.   [3] B om.
[4] Blessed is he who has given a just judgement, and assists the orphan
and the widow, and every one who is oppressed : clothes the naked,
and gives bread to the hungry, B.   [5] Path of deceit, B.

---

beatitudes.   These are very colourless.   7. Executes a just judgement.   Cf. ix; Ezek. xviii. 8.   This
verse recalls in some measure the
words of Antigonus of Socho : 'Be
not like servants who serve their
master for the sake of reward, but be
like those who do service without
respect to recompense, and live always in the fear of God.'   Expecting
nothing in return.   Cf. Luke vi.
35.   Sincere.   Corrupt.   With the
entire verse we have a good parallel
in Orac. Sibyll. ii. 61, 63

πάντα δίκαια νέμειν, μηδ' εἰς ἄδικον
    κρίσιν ἐλθῆς.
ἢν σὺ κακῶς δικάσῃς, σὲ θεὸς μετέ-
    πειτα δικάσσει.

8. These words are found in ix.
9. Cf. ix ; Ps. x. 18 ; Is. i. 17 ; Jer.
xxii. 3, 16 ; Zech. vii. 9, 10.   10.

Walks by the righteous path.   Cf.
Prov. iv. 11 ; Or Sibyll. iii. 9-10

τίπτε . . . οὐκ εὐθεῖαν ἀταρπὸν
βαίνετε ἀθανάτου κτιστοῦ μεμνημένοι
    αἰεί :

also Fragm. i. 23 sq.   11. Is the
blessing for those who sow seed that
is justly their own ?   In Orac. Sibyll.
ii. 71-72, 'he who steals seed is
accursed for ever' :

σπέρματα μὴ κλέπτειν· ἐπαράσιμος
    ὅς τις ἕληται
ἐς γενεὰς γενεῶν, ἐς σκορπισμὸν
    βιότοιο.

On the other hand, the reference may
be metaphorical and the sense as follows : 'From your righteous deeds ye
will reap sevenfold.'   This is probably
an adaptation of Ecclus. vii. 3 μὴ σπεῖρε
ἐπ' αὔλακας ἀδικίας, καὶ οὐ μὴ θερίσῃς
αὐτὰς ἐπταπλασίως.   Cf. Job iv. 8;

he shall reap sevenfold. 12. Blessed is he in whom is the truth, that he may speak the truth to *his neighbour[1]. 13. Blessed is he * who has love upon his lips, and tenderness in his heart[2]. 14. Blessed is he who understands every work of the Lord, *and glorifies the Lord God[3]; *for the works of the Lord are just, and of the works of man some are good, and others evil, and by their works those who have wrought them are known[4].

[*Enoch shows his Children how he measured and wrote out the Judgements of God.*]

XLIII. 1. *Lo! my children, the things which I have gained on the earth and meditated upon from the Lord God I have written down both winter and summer. I have compiled the account of all, and concerning the years I have calculated each hour; I have measured the hours and written out the lists of them and I have ascertained all their differences[5]. 2. As one year is more honourable than another[6], so is one man more honourable than another. This

---

[1] The man who is sincere, Sok. [2] Upon whose lips are tenderness and mercy, B. [3] Accomplished by the Lord and glorifies him, Sok. [4] B om. A reads And I saw all the works of the Lord how righteous they are, and of the works of men some (are righteous) but others wicked. And the impure are known by their deeds.

XLIII. [5] I, my children, have measured and written out every deed and every measure, and every just judgement (weight, Sok.), A Sok. Sok. adds: And have written them out as the Lord ordered me, and in all these I have found diversity. [6] B adds and one day more than another and one hour more than another.

Prov. xxii. 8; Hos. x. 13. 12. Cf. Lev. xix. 11; Eph. iv. 25; Orac. Sibyll. ii. 58 ψεύδεα μὴ βάζειν: 64 μαρτυρίην ψευδῆ φεύγειν, τὰ δίκαι' ἀγορεύειν. 13. Cf. Prov. xxxi. 26. 14. By their works ... are known. Cf. Mt. vii. 16, 20.

XLIII. 2, 3. As one year, &c. We should expect rather as one day, &c. Cf. Ecclus. xxiii. 7 διὰ τί ἡμέρα ἡμέρας ὑπερέχει; The main thought of these verses is derived from Ecclus. x. 20, 22, 24 (cf. Jer. ix. 23, 24): in

fact no one is greater than he who fears God is a direct quotation from x. 24. This passage runs: 20 ἐν μέσῳ ἀδελφῶν ὁ ἡγούμενος αὐτῶν ἔντιμος, καὶ οἱ φοβούμενοι κύριον ἐν ὀφθαλμοῖς αὐτοῦ. 22. πλούσιος καὶ ἔνδοξος καὶ πτωχός, τὸ καύχημα αὐτῶν φόβος κυρίου. 24. μεγιστὰν καὶ κριτὴς καὶ δυνάστης δοξασθήσεται, καὶ οὐκ ἔστιν αὐτῶν τις μείζων τοῦ φοβουμένου τὸν κύριον. ... 30. πτωχὸς δοξάζεται δι' ἐπιστήμην αὐτοῦ, καὶ πλούσιος δοξάζεται διὰ τὸν πλοῦτον αὐτοῦ. Cf. Orac. Sibyll. ii. 125.

man on account of many possessions, that man on account
of the wisdom [1] of the heart; this man on account of understanding, another on account of cunning; this man for the
silence of the lips [2]; * this man on account of purity, that on
account of strength; this man on account of comeliness,
another on account of youth; this man on account of sharpness of mind, another on account of quicksightedness of body,
and another for the perception of many things.   3. Let it
be heard everywhere [3]; there is no one greater than he who
fears God.   He shall be the most glorious for ever.

*[Enoch instructs his Sons that they should not revile the Persons
of Men, whether they are great or small.]*

XLIV. 1. God [4] made man with His own hands, in the
likeness of His countenance, both small and great the Lord
created him.   He who reviles the countenance of * man,
reviles the countenance of the Lord [5].   2. * He who shows
wrath against another without injury, the great wrath of the
Lord shall consume him.   3. If a man spits at the face of
another [6] * insultingly, he shall be consumed [7] * in the great
judgement of the Lord [8].   4. Blessed is the man who * does
not direct his heart with malice against any [9] man, and who
assists the man who is * injured, and [10] under judgement, and
raises up the oppressed, * and accomplishes the prayer of him
who asks [11]!   5. For in the day of the great judgement,

----

[1] Benevolence, B.   [2] Tongue and lips, B.   [3] B om.
XLIV. [4] B adds fashioned and.   [5] The prince, and loathes the
countenance of the Lord; despises the countenance of the Lord, A.
Man reviles the countenance of the prince and loathes the counte-
ance of the Lord, Sok.   [6] There is the anger of the Lord, and a great
judgement for whoever spits in the face of a man, B.   [7] His insolence
will consume him, Sok.; B om.   [8] B om.   [9] Puts confidence in, B.
[10] A, Sok. om.   [11] Performs a kindness to him who wants it, Sok.; B om.

XLIV. 1. He who reviles the
countenance, &c.   We may reasonably compare James iii. 9.   2. Cf.

Matt. v. 22.   4. This beatitude
seems out of place here.   It would
come in fittingly at the close of xlii.

every measure and standard and weight, * which is for traffic,
namely, that which is hung on a balance and stands for
traffic[1], knows its own measure, and * shall receive its
reward by measure[2].

[*God shows that He does not wish Sacrifices from Man, nor
Burnt-Offerings, but pure and contrite Hearts.*]   .

XLV. 1. * He who hastens and brings his offering before
the face of the Lord, then the Lord will hasten the accomplish-
ment of his work, and will execute a just judgement for him[3].
2. He who increases his lamp before the face of the Lord, the
Lord increases greatly his treasure *in the heavenly kingdom[4].
3. God does not require bread, nor a light, * nor an animal,
nor any other sacrifice[5], * for it is as nothing[6].   4. * But
God requires a pure heart[4], and by means of all this, He tries
the heart of man.

---

[1] **Hang as on a balance, that is on the scale and which stands for
traffic, Sok.   B OMITS ENTIRE VERSE.**   [2] **Its measure shall receive its
reward, Sok.**
XLV. [3] **If a man hastens to work folly before the Lord, the Lord
furthers him in the carrying out of his work, and makes his judgement
faulty. So A through a corruption of приносъ into прасно and insertion of
не before сотворить; B om.**   [4] **B om.**   [5] **Nor food of any kind nor
meat, B.   Nor an animal, nor an ox, nor any other victim, Sok.**   [6] **That
is not so, Sok.; B om.**

- - - - - - - -

XLV. 3. Cf. Ps. xl. 6; li. 16;
Is. i. 11; Mic. vi. 6–8; Eccl. xxxii.
1–3; Orac. Sibyll. viii. 390, 391
οὐ χρήζω θυσίης ἢ σπονδῆς ὑμετέ-
ρῃφιν
οὐ κνίσσης μαρῆς, οὐχ αἵματος ἐχθί-
στοιο:
also ii. 82; Athenag. *Supplic. pro
Christo*, 13. This is not Essenism:
see lix. 1–3. We find the same
spiritual appreciation of sacrifices in

Ecclus. xxxii. 1–5 side by side with
injunctions to offer them: ὁ συντη-
ρῶν νόμον πλεονάζει προσφοράς, θυσιάζων σωτηρίου ὁ προσέχων ἐντολαῖς ἀντα-
ποδιδοὺς χάριν προσφέρων σεμίδαλιν,
καὶ ὁ ποιῶν ἐλεημοσύναν θυσιάζων αἰ-
νέσεως καὶ ἐξιλασμὸς ἀποστῆναι ἀπὸ
πονηρίας.   4. **A pure heart.** Ps.
li. 10. **Tries the heart of man.**
Deut. viii. 2; 2 Chron. xxxii. 31;
Ps. xxvi. 2.

[*How an earthly Prince will not receive Gifts from Man which
are contemptible and impure. How much more does God
loath impure Gifts, and rejects them with Wrath, and will
not receive the Gifts of such a Man.*]

XLVI. 1. * Hear, my people, and pay attention to the
words of my lips [1]. If any one brings gifts to an earthly
prince, but having unfaithfulness in his heart: if the prince
knows it, will he not be angry with * him on account of that,
and he will not take [2] his gifts, and will hand him over to
condemnation?   2. Or if a man flatters another * in his
language, but (plans) evil against him in his heart, will not
the other understand the craft of his heart, and he himself
will be condemned, so that his unrighteousness will be evi-
dent to all [3]?   3. But when God shall send a great light, by
means of that there will be judgement [4] to the just and
unjust, and nothing will be concealed.

[*Enoch instructs his Sons from the Lips of God, and gives
them the Manuscripts of this Book.*]

XLVII. 1. Now, my children, put my thoughts in your
hearts; pay attention to the words of your father, which
* have come to [5] you from the mouth of the Lord.   2. Take
these books of the writings of your father, and read them,
* and in them ye shall learn all the works of the Lord.
There have been many books from the beginning of creation,
and shall be to the end of the world, but none shall make

XLVI. [1] Sok. om. B OMITS ENTIRE CHAPTER.   [2] Sok. om.   [3] With
falsehood and is good in his tongue but evil in his heart, will not his
heart perceive this and he will judge by himself so that he is proved not
to be right, Sok.   [4] Just judgement that is no respecter of persons, Sok.
XLVII. [5] I tell, Sok. B OMITS ENTIRE CHAPTER.

XLVI. 2. Cf. Orac. Sibyll. ii. 120
μηδ' ἕτερον κεύθοις κραδίῃ νόον ἀλλ'
ἀγορεύων.   3. What the great

light means is not clear.
XLVII. 1. Cf. xxxix. 2.   2.
None shall make things known

things known to you like my writings [1]. 3. But if you
shall preserve [2] my writings, you will not sin against God.
For there is no other besides the Lord, neither in heaven nor
on earth, nor the depths below, nor the solitary foundations.
4. God established the foundations upon things that are
unknown, and stretched out the *visible and invisible
heavens [3], and made firm the earth upon the waters,
and established the waters on things that are not fixed [4].
Who has created all the innumerable works of creation?
5. *Who has numbered the dust of the earth [5], and the sand
of the sea, and the drops of rain, and the dew of the morning,
*and the breath of the wind [6]? Who has *bound earth and
sea with bonds [7] that cannot be broken up: *and has cut [8] the
stars out of fire, *and beautified [9] the heavens [10], and placed
* the sun [11] in the midst of them * so that [11].

[*Of the course of the Sun throughout the seven Circles.*]
XLVIII. 1. The sun [12] goes in the seven circles of the

---

[1] For the books are many and in them we shall learn all the words
of the Lord. Such as they are from the beginning of creation, so shall
they be to the end of the world, A.   [2] Keep strictly, Sok.   [3] Heavens
over the visible things, Sok.   [4] A reads And He considered what
is the water and the foundation of things that are not stedfast and,
and transposes these words to end of verse.   [6] Sok. om.   [7] Has filled earth
and sea and the winter, A.   [8] Emended from And I cut, A; and (who)
sowed, Sok.   [9] And I beautified, A.   [10] Sok. adds and placed.   [11] A om.
XLVIII. [12] He, Sok.

---

to you like my writings. Cf. Eth.
En. xciii. 10.   3. But... not sin
against God. Cf. xxxiii. 9; xlviii.
7–9. This claim is analogous to that
made in the Eth. En. xxxvii. 4; xcii. 1;
xciii. 10; c. 6; civ. 12, 13. With this
we may contrast Ecclus. xviii. 3 οὐθενὶ
ἐξεποίησεν ἐξαγγεῖλαι τὰ ἔργα αὐτοῦ.
There is no other besides the Lord.
Cf. Is. xlv. 5, 14, 18, 22. This is a
favourite sentiment in the Sibylline
Oracles. Cf. iii. 69

αὐτὸς γὰρ μόνος ἐστὶ θεὸς κοὐκ
ἔστιν ἔτ' ἄλλος:

also iii. 760; viii. 377; Fragm. i. 7,
15; iii. 3; v. 1.   4. Stretched

out, &c. Ps. civ. 2; Is. xl. 22; xlii.
5. Made firm the earth upon the
waters, 2 Pet. iii. 5.   5. Who has
numbered... the sand of the sea,
and the drops of rain. This is
drawn word for word from Ecclus.
i. 2 ἄμμον θαλασσῶν καὶ σταγόνας
ὑετοῦ . . . τίς ἐξαριθμήσει; Cf. Is.
xl. 12, and the oracle in Herod. i. 47
οἶδα δ' ἐγὼ ψάμμου τ' ἀριθμὸν καὶ
μέτρα θαλάσσης, and likewise recalls
LXX Job xxxvi. 27 ἀριθμηταὶ δὲ
αὐτῷ σταγόνες ὑετοῦ. Beautified
the heavens. Cf. Ecclus. xvi. 27
ἐκόσμησεν εἰς αἰῶνα τὰ ἔργα αὐτοῦ.

XLVIII. 1. The text is corrupt

heavens, * and I gave him [1] 182 thrones when he goes
on a short day, and also 182 thrones when he goes on a long
day.   2. And he has two great thrones on which he rests,
returning hither and thither above the monthly thrones.
From the month Tsivan [2] after [3] seventeen days he descends
to the month Thevan [4], and from the seventeenth day of
Thevad [4] he ascends.   3. And so the sun goes through
all the courses of the heaven [3]; when he goes near the earth,
then the earth rejoices and produces its fruit; when he
departs, then the earth is sad, and the trees and all the fruits
have no development.   4. *All this by measure and minute
arrangement of time He has arranged by His wisdom [5], both
in the case of things visible and invisible.   5. He has
made all things visible out of invisible, Himself being
invisible.   6. Thus I tell you, my children, distribute the
books to your children, in all your families, and among the
nations.   7. Those who are wise let them fear God, and
let them receive them * and let them love them more than

---

[1] Which are the support of the, A. B OMITS ENTIRE CHAPTER.
[2] Pamorus, Sok.   [3] A om.   [4] Thibith, Sok.   [5] Hereby he gives
a complete measure and with good arrangement of the times and has
fixed a measure, A.

---

and unintelligible. According to xi.
1; xxx. 3 the sun is in the fourth
circle of the heavens and does not
revolve through the seven circles.
Again the twice-mentioned 182 thrones
are really when added the 364 world-
stations of which we have some
account in the Eth. En. lxxv. 2, i.e.
'the harmony of the course of the
world is brought about through its
separate 364 world-stations.' These
world-stations or **thrones** as in our
text are the 364 different positions
occupied by the sun on the 364 days
of the year. Just as in the Eth. En.
lxxii – lxxxii and Jubilees iv no
attempt is made here to get the
complete number of days in the solar

year, i.e. 365¼: contrast xiv. 1. This
passage therefore either belongs to or
is built upon the oldest literature of
Enoch. This reckoning of the year
at 364 days may be due partly to
opposition to heathen systems and
partly to the fact that 364 is divisible
by 7, and amounts to 52 weeks
exactly. See Eth. En. 190-91.   2.
Tsivan . . . Thevad. The text is
here corrupt. As apparently the two
solstices are meant, we should read
either **Sivan . . . Kislev** or **Tamuz
. . . Tebet.**   5. Cf. xxiv. 2 (note);
xlvii. 2 (note). Has made here was
no doubt ἔπλασε, not ἐποίησε.   6. See
xxxiii. 9 (note).   7. **Let them love
them more than any kind of food.**

any kind of food [1], and read them [2].   8. * But those who are senseless and have no thought of the Lord and do not fear God [3] will not receive them but turn away, and * keep themselves from them [4], * the terrible judgement shall await them [5]. 9. Blessed is the man who bears their yoke, and puts it on, for he shall be set free in the day of the great judgement.

[*Enoch instructs his Sons not to swear either by the Heaven or the Earth ; and shows the Promise of God to a Man even in the Womb of his Mother.*]

XLIX. 1. For [5] I swear to you my children [6], but I will not swear by a single oath, neither by heaven, nor by earth, nor by any other creature which God made.   God [7] said : 'There

---

[1] And the books will be more profitable to them than all good food on earth, Sok. A adds or earthly advantage.   [2] Sok. adds And let them cling to them.   [3] And it shall result to them if they have no thought of God nor fear him, and if they, A.   [4] Do not receive the books, A.   [5] Sok. om.
XLIX. [6] B om. rest of verse.   [7] For the Lord, Sok.

So Eth. En. lxxxii. 3 'this wisdom will please those that eat (thereof) better than good food.' Cf. xlvii. 2 (note).   8. Those who . . . will not receive them . . . the terrible judgement shall await them. The punishment denounced against those who refuse the disclosures of this book is more severe than anything to be found in the Eth. En. For a perfect parallel we must go to Rev. xxii. 18, 19.   9. The appeal for reception is far wider in this book than in the Eth. En. There only 'the elect of righteousness,' 'the righteous and the wise,' 'those who understand,' receive the revelations of Enoch: cf. lxxxii. 3 ; xciii. 10; civ. 12.   Bears their yoke, cf. xxxiv. 1.

XLIX. 1. Swear . . . neither by heaven, &c. From this passage and

from Philo it is clear that Mt. v. 34–35 was a Jewish commonplace. For in Philo *de Special. Leg.* ii. 1 we find: ὁ γὰρ τοῦ σπουδαίου, φησί, λόγος ὅρκος ἔστω βέβαιος, ἀκλινής, ἀψευδέστατος, ἐρηρεισμένος ἀληθείᾳ . . . εἰώθασι γὰρ ἀναφθεγξάμενοι τοσοῦτον μόνον 'νὴ τόν,' ἤ 'μὰ τόν,' μηδὲν παραλαβόντες, ἐμφάσει τῆς ἀποκοπῆς, τρανοῦν ὅρκον οὐ γενόμενον. 'Αλλὰ καὶ παραλαβέτω τις, εἰ βούλοιτο, μὴ μὴν τὸ ἀνωτάτω καὶ πρεσβύτατον εὐθὺς αἴτιον, ἀλλὰ γῆν, ἥλιον, ἀστέρας, οὐρανόν, τὸν σύμπαντα κόσμον: *De decem Orac.* 17 Κάλλιστον δὴ καὶ βιωφελέστατον καὶ ἁρμόττον λογικῇ φύσει τὸ ἀνώμοτον, οὕτως ἀληθεύειν ἐφ' ἑκάστου δεδιδαγμένῃ, ὡς τοὺς λόγους ὅρκους εἶναι νομίζεσθαι. Cp. also *Leg. All.* iii. 72; *De Sac. Abelis et Caini,* 28; *De Plant. Noe* 19; *Quod Omnis Probus Liber,* 12. It was Mr. Conybeare

is no swearing in me, nor injustice, but truth. If there is
no truth in men, let them swear by a word, yea, yea, or nay,
nay.   2. * But I swear to you, yea, yea [1], that * there has
not been even a man in his mother's womb, for whom a place
has not been prepared for every soul [2]; * and a measure is fixed
how long a man shall be tried in this world [3]. * O! my
children, be not deceived [1] * there is a place prepared there
for every soul of man [4].

[*How Nobody born upon the Earth can hide himself, nor are his
Deeds concealed. (God) commands that he should be on the
Earth a short time, endure Temptation, and Annoyance, and
not injure the Widow and Orphan.*]

L. 1. I have laid down in the writings the actions of every
man, * and no one born on the earth can hide himself, nor can
his deeds be concealed ; I see all [5].   2. Now, therefore, my
children, in patience and meekness accomplish the number
of your days, and ye shall inherit the endless life which is to
come.   3. * Every wound, and every affliction, and every

---

[1] B om.   [2] So A Sok. but that for every A reads the rest of
that. B reads Even before man was created a place of judgement was
prepared for him.   [3] And a measure and a standard how long a man
shall live in this world, and shall be tried in it, Sok. ; And it was measured out and fixed, and there man will be tried, B.   [4] So A Sok. but
that Sok. adds previously after place. B reads As before it was appointed
for him.
L. [5] B om. ; Sok. adds as in a looking-glass.

---

that first called my attention to
these passages in Philo. On the
various forms of swearing usual
among the Jews and censured in
Mt. v. 33–36 and indirectly in the
text, see Lightfoot *in loc.*; Eisenmenger, ii. 490 sqq.
    XLIX. 2. A place ... prepared
for every soul. So *Tractat Chagiga*,
fol. 15, col. 1 ; *Torath Adam*, fol. 101,
col. 3 ; *Avodath hakkodesh*, fol. 19,
col. 1, where it is said that a place

is prepared for every man either in
Paradise or Hell (Eisenmenger, ii.
315).
    L. 1. Nor can his deeds be con-
cealed. Eth. En. ix. 5. 2. In
patience, &c. Cp. Luke xxi. 19
' In your patience ye shall win your
souls.' A blessed immortality for the
righteous is taught in this book, but
apparently no resurrection of the
body. 3. Cp. Ecclus. ii. 4 ; 2 Tim.
iv. 5 ; Heb. x. 32 ; 1 Pet. ii. 19 ;

evil word, and attack¹ endure for the sake of the Lord.
4. And when you might have vengeance² do not repay, either
*your neighbour or your enemy³. For God⁴ will repay as
your avenger in the *day of the great judgement⁵. *Let it
not be for you to take vengeance⁶. 5. Whoever of you
shall spend gold or silver for the sake of a brother, shall receive
abundant treasure in *the day of judgement⁷ *and stretch
out your hands to⁸ the orphan, the widow, and the stranger⁹.

[*Enoch instructs his Sons, not to hide their Treasures upon
Earth, but bids them give Alms to the Needy.*]

LI. 1. *Stretch out your hands to the poor man¹⁰ according
to your powers. 2. *Do not hide your silver in the earth¹¹ :

---

¹ Whatever wound or disease or affliction or evil end shall light
upon you, B. Put away from you every wound and every injury and
every evil word. If an attack and an injury be inflicted upon you for
the sake of the Lord, Sok. ² Sok. adds an hundredfold. ³ Your
neighbour, B; one who is near you or afar off, Sok. ⁴ Living
God, B; Lord, Sok. ⁵ Great day of, A. ⁶ Therefore be not
avenged here from men but then from the Lord, Sok. B om. ⁷ That
world, A Sok. ⁸ Do not oppress, A. ⁹ B om.; A adds lest the
wrath of God should come upon you.
LI. ¹⁰ And assist the poor man, B; Sok. om. ¹¹ Sok. reads in your
treasures after come upon you, B om.

Jam. i. 12. See li. 3. 4. Cp. Ecclus.
xxviii. 1 ὁ ἐκδικῶν παρὰ Κυρίου
εὑρήσει ἐκδίκησιν, καὶ τὰς ἁμαρτίας
αὐτοῦ διαστηρῶν διαστηρίσει. 2. ἄφες
ἀδίκημα τῷ πλησίον σου, καὶ τότε
δεηθέντος σου αἱ ἁμαρτίαι σου λυθήσον-
ται. See also verses 3-6. God will
repay ... in the day of the great
judgement. These words follow the
LXX of Deut. xxxii. 35 ἐν ἡμέρᾳ
ἐκδικήσεως ἀνταποδώσω. The LXX
thus read ליום נקם אשלם instead of
the Mass. נקם שלם לי. The
Samaritan likewise reads ליום. Cp.
also Prov. xx. 22; xxiv. 29. In
Rom. xii. 19; Heb. x. 30, the writers
follow a text of Deut. xxxii. 35 agree-
ing partly with the Mass. and partly

with that implied by the LXX. 5.
Whoever, &c. Cp. Prov. xix. 17 :
Ecclus. xxix. 10. See LI. 2 (note).
Stretch out your hands to the
orphan, &c. Orac. Sibyll. ii. 75
ὀρφανικοῖς χήραις τ' ἐπιδευομένοις τε
παράσχου. Cf. ix.
LI. 1. Stretch out your hands
to the poor, &c. This is drawn
from Ecclus. vii. 32 πτωχῷ ἔκτεινον
τὴν χεῖρά σου, which in turn seems
drawn from Prov. xxxi. 20. Cf. Job
vii. 9: Orac. Sibyll. ii. 88. According to your powers. Cf.
Ecclus. xiv. 13; xxix. 20. 2. Do
not hide your silver in the earth.
Cf. Ecclus. xxix. 10 ἀπόλεσον ἀργύριον
δι' ἀδελφὸν καὶ φίλον καὶ μὴ ἰωθήτω ὑπὸ

*assist the honest man in his affliction, and affliction shall not come upon you, in the time of your labour. 3. And whatever violent and grievous yoke shall be put upon you, endure all for the Lord's sake[1], and so you will receive your reward in the day of judgement.   4. Morning, afternoon, and evening, it is good to go into the house of the Lord to glorify *the Creator of all[2].   5. Wherefore[3] let every thing that hath breath glorify Him, and let every creature visible and invisible give forth praise.

[*God instructs His faithful Servants how they are to praise His Name.*]

LII. 1. Blessed is the man who opens *his lips to praise the God of Sabaoth, and praises the Lord with his heart[4]. 2. Cursed is every man who opens his *lips to abuse and to calumniate his neighbour[5].   3. Blessed[6] is he who opens his lips to the blessing and praise of God!   4. Cursed is he who opens his lips to swearing and blasphemy before the face of the Lord all his days.   5. Blessed is he who

---

[1] B om.   [2] Your Creator, A.   [3] For, Sok.; Sok. also puts the verbs in the indicative; B OMITS VERSE.
    LII. [4] Heart and lips to the praise of the Lord, B.   [5] Heart to abuse, abusing the poor and calumniating his neighbour, Sok.; B supports text but that it omits and to calumniate.   After neighbour A adds for him shall God rebuke.   [6] B OMITS VERSES 3, 4.

τὸν λίθον. Assist ... in his affliction. Cf. Ecclus. iv. 4 ἱκέτην θλιβόμενον μὴ ἀπαναίνου. 3. Ecclus. ii. 4 πᾶν ὃ ἐὰν ἐπαχθῇ σοι . . . μακροθύμησον. Cf. I Pet. ii. 19; iii. 14. Cf. L. 3. 4. Ps. lv. 17: Cf. Dan. vi. 10. These three Jewish hours of prayer—the *third* (that of morning sacrifice), the *sixth* (noon), the *ninth* (that of evening sacrifice)—are observed in Acts ii. 15; iii. 1; x. 9. See Lightfoot *in loc.* for his Talmudic references. House of the Lord. This means the temple; for though the author is a Jew living in Egypt, he is writing for Judaism as a whole, and is giving herein the ideal conduct of an inhabitant of Jerusalem. In LIX. 2, 3, he prescribes the right method of sacrifice, and sacrifices could only be offered in Jerusalem. 5. Every thing that, &c. Ps. cl. 6.

LII. With these beatitudes compare xlii. 6–14. Like the latter these are wanting in vigour. They seem to be in the main derived from Ecclesiasticus. 2. Cf. Wisdom i. 11 ἀπὸ καταλαλιᾶς φείσασθε γλώσσης. 4 Swearing and blasphemy. Cf. Ecclus. xxiii. 9–12. 5. Cf. Ecclus.

blesses all the works of the Lord.   6. Cursed is he who speaks ill of [1] the works of the Lord.   7. Blessed is he who *looks to raise his own hand for labour [2].   8. Cursed is he who looks to [3] make use of another man's labour.   9. Blessed is he who preserves the foundations of his fathers *from the beginning [4].   10. Cursed is he who breaks the enactments [5] of his fathers.   11. Blessed is he who *establishes peace and love [6].   12. Cursed is he who troubles those who *are at peace [7].   13. Blessed is he who *does not speak peace with his tongue, but in his heart there is peace to all [8]!   14. Cursed is he who speaks peace with his tongue, but in his heart there is no peace [9].   15. For all these things in measures and in books will be revealed in the day of the great judgement [10].

[*Let us not say that our Father is with God, and will plead for us at the Day of Judgement. For I know that a Father cannot help his Son, nor a Son a Father.*]

LIII. 1. And now, my children, do not say ; Our father

---

[1] Sok. adds all.   [2] **Looks to the work of his own hands, B. Looks to raise up the fallen, A.**   [3] A adds and is eager to.   [4] B om.
[5] B adds and ordinances.   [6] Goes to seek peace and leads others to peace, B.   [7] **Love their neighbours, A.**   [8] Speaks peace, for peace abides with him, B.   **Speaks with a humble tongue and heart to all, A.**   [9] A adds a sword. B OMITS ENTIRE VERSE.
[10] B adds **Therefore, my brethren, preserve your hearts from everything unjust that you may inherit an habitation of light for ever.**

---

xxxix. 14 εὐλογήσατε κύριον ἐπὶ πᾶσι τοῖς ἔργοις αὐτοῦ. 7. Cf. Eph. iv. 28. 8. Seems to be derived from Ecclus. xxxi. 26 φονεύων τὸν πλησίον ὁ ἀφαιρούμενος συμβίωσιν, καὶ ἐκχέων αἷμα ὁ ἀποστερῶν μίσθον μισθίου. Cf. Orac. Sibyll. ii. 56–57 :

μὴ πλουτεῖν ἀδίκως, ἀλλ' ἐξ ὁσίων βιοτεύειν.
ἀρκεῖσθαι παρεοῦσι· καὶ ἀλλοτρίων ἀπέχεσθαι.

10. Cf. Eth. En. xcix. 2, 14 ; Ecclus. xvii. 11. 11. Cf. Mt. v. 9. 12. This is derived from Ecclus. xxviii. 9 ἀνὴρ

ἁμαρτωλὸς ταράξει φίλους καὶ ἀνὰ μέσον εἰρηνευόντων ἐκβάλλει διαβολήν. Cf. also Ecclus. xxviii. 13. 14. Cf. Ps. xxviii. 3; lv. 21; lxii. 4; Orac. Sibyll. ii. 120, 122.

LIII. 1. This idea that departed saints interceded on behalf of the living has been attributed by some scholars to Is. lxiii. 16 (see Ewald, *History of Israel*, i. 296; Cheyne, *Prophecies of Isaiah*, ii. 107–108; 299–300). If, however, the doctrine of a blessed immortality or of the resurrection was a late development

stands before God, and prays * for us (to be released) from sin [1]; * for there is no person there to help any man who has sinned [2].   2. You see how I have written down all the works of every man * before his creation [2], * which is [3] * done in the case of all men for ever [2].   3. And no man * can say or unsay [4] what I have written with my hand.   For God sees all things, * even the thoughts of wicked men [5], * which lie in the storeplaces of the heart [2].   4. And now,

---

LIII. [1] Concerning our sins, A. what things are, Sok.; B om. [5] The thoughts of man that they are vain, A; B om. [2] B om. [3] And I shall write [4] Destroy, B; contradict, Sok.

---

among the Jews, this idea must necessarily have been later still, and accordingly unless we are prepared to bring down considerably the date of Is. lxiii, we shall have some difficulty in justifying such an interpretation. It seems indeed that this idea among the Jews was comparatively late in origin. The first indubitable evidence in its favour is to be found in the Eth. En. xxii. 12; xcvii. 3, 5; xcix. 16; and thus we find that it was an accepted Pharisaic belief early in the second century B.C. The next mention of this belief is to be met with in 2 Macc. xv. 14 where Jeremiah, who appears in a vision to Judas Maccabaeus, is described as follows: ὁ φιλάδελφος οὗτός ἐστιν ὁ πολλὰ προσευχόμενος περὶ τοῦ λαοῦ καὶ τῆς ἁγίας πόλεως Ἰερεμίας ὁ τοῦ θεοῦ προφήτης. This was also the teaching of Philo, de Exsecrat. 9: τρισὶ χρησόμενοι παρακλήτοις τῶν πρὸς τὸν πατέρα καταλλαγῶν . . . δευτέρῳ δὲ τῇ τῶν ἀρχηγετῶν τοῦ ἔθνους ὁσιότητι, ὅτι ταῖς ἀφειμέναις σωμάτων ψυχαῖς ἄπλαστον καὶ γυμνὴν ἐπιδεικνυμέναις πρὸς τὸν ἄρχοντα θεραπείαν τὰς ὑπὲρ υἱῶν καὶ θυγατέρων ἱκετείας οὐκ ἀτελεῖς εἰώθασι ποιεῖσθαι, γέρας αὐτοῖς παρέχοντος τοῦ πατρὸς τὸ ἐπήκοον ἐν εὐχαῖς. The

same view was obviously held by Joseph. *Antt.* i. 13. 3, where he describes Abraham as saying to Isaac when on the point of sacrificing him: μετ' εὐχῶν δὲ καὶ ἱερουργίας ἐκείνου τὴν ψυχὴν τὴν σὴν προσδεξομένου καὶ παρ' αὐτῷ καθέξοντος ἔσῃ μοὶ εἰς κηδεμόνα καὶ γηροκόμον. And also in Orac. Sibyll. ii. 330–333:

τοῖς καὶ ὁ παντοκράτωρ θεὸς ἄφθιτος
 ἄλλο παρέξει
εὐσεβέεσσ', ὁπότ' ἂν θεὸν ἄφθιτον
 αἰτήσωνται·
ἐκ μαλεροῖο πυρός τε καὶ ἀκαμάτων
 ἀπὸ βρυγμῶν
ἀνθρώπους σῶσαι δώσει· καὶ τοῦτο
 ποιήσει.

Finally this doctrine is recognized and apparently accepted in certain parts of the N. T.: Matt. xxvii. 47, 49; Luke xvi. 24–31; John viii. 56 (?); Heb. xii. 1 ?; Rev. vi. 9–11. For the prevalence of this belief in later Judaism, see Eisenmenger, ii. 357–9; 361. The idea of intercession may be derived from ancestor-worship, and not from the doctrine of a future life as I have implied above; cf. Cheyne's *Introd. to the Book of Isaiah*, 352, 3. 2. Enoch is the universal scribe. 3. Cf. Ps. xciv. 11; Ecclus. xvii. 15. 20.

my children, pay attention to all the words * of your father
which I say to you[1] : * that ye may not grieve afterwards
and say : Our father for some cause or other, never told them
to us, in the time of this folly[2].

[*Enoch admonishes his Sons that they should give the Books
to Others.*]

LIV. * Let these books which I have given you be the
inheritance of your peace[3] : * do not conceal them[4] but tell[5]
them to all desiring them * and admonish them[6] that * they
may know the works of the Lord which are very wonderful[7].

[*Here Enoch makes a Declaration to his Sons: and speaks to
them with Tears: 'My children, my Hour draws near, that
I should go to Heaven. Lo! Angels stand before me!'*]

LV. 1. My children, the appointed day and time[8] have drawn
near * and constrain me to depart[9]. The angels * will come
and[10] stand before me * on the earth awaiting what has
been ordered them[11].　　2. In the morning I shall go to the
highest[12] heavens[13] to my eternal habitation.　　3. Therefore
I tell you to do all that is good before the face of the Lord.

[*Methosalem asks a Blessing of his Father; that he may
give him Bread to eat.*]

LVI. 1. Methosalem having answered his father Enoch
said[14] : 'If it is good in thine eyes, * my father[15],* let me

---

[1] Of the lips of your father, B.　　[2] B om.
　　LIV. [3] That you may have an inheritance of peace and the books
which I have given you from God, B.　[4] A om.　[5] Give, A.　[6] Sok.
om.　[7] Words cannot make known the works of God, B.
　　LV. [8] B adds appointed by God.　　[9] A reads after stand before
me.　　[10] Who wish to-go with me, A Sok.　　[11] So A Sok. but that
before on the earth, A adds they now stand; B om.　　[12] Upper, B ;
A om.　　[13] A adds to the highest Jerusalem.
　　LVI. [14] B om.　　[15] Enoch, Sok.

LIV. See xxxiii. 9 (note). Works　　LV. 1. See xxxvi.　　2. Highest
... wonderful. Job xxxvii. 14, 16 ;　heavens. Cf. lxvii. 2.
Ps. lxxi. 17, &c.

put food [1] before thy face and then, having blessed our houses and thy sons, * and all thy family [2], let thy people be glorified by thee; and then afterwards thou wilt depart, * as God hath said [3].'   2. Enoch answered his son * Methosalem and said [4]: 'Hear my child, since God has anointed me with the oil of his glory, there has been no [2] food in me, * and my soul remembers nothing of earthly pleasure [5] nor do I desire * anything earthly [6].

[*Enoch orders his Son Methosalem to call all his Brothers.*]

LVII. 1. But [7] call all [8] thy brothers, and all your [9] families, and the elders of the people, that I may speak to them and depart * as is appointed for me [8].   2. And Methosalem hastened, and called his brethren, Regim, Riman [10], Ukhan [11], Khermion, [Gaidal [8]], and [12] the elders of [13] the people, * and brought them all [14] before the face of his father Enoch [15]. And having blessed them, he spake to them [16].

[*The Instruction of Enoch to his Sons.*]

LVIII. 1. 'Listen to me, my sons. * In those days when the Lord came upon the earth for the sake of Adam, and visited [17] all his creation, which He Himself had made [18]. 2. The [19] Lord [20] called all the cattle of the earth [21], and all

---

[1] Let me do, A : let us put food, Sok. Sok.; B om.   [4] And said, Sok.; B om.   [2] A om.   [3] As God wishes, [5] B om.   [6] Earthly food, B.
    LVII. [7] My son Methosalem, A.   [8] B om.   [9] Our, B.   [10] Rim, B.   [11] Azukhan, B.   [12] A adds all.   [13] Sok. adds all.   [14] And called them, Sok.; A om.   [15] Sok. adds and they bowed before his face, and Enoch saw them.   [16] Sok. adds saying.
    LVIII. [17] So A and Sok., but that Sok. adds your father after Adam ; B reads in the days of our father Adam the Lord came to visit him and.   [18] A adds and after all these created Adam : Sok. adds in brackets in the previous thousand years and after all these created Adam.   [19] And the, A B Sok.   [20] Lord God, B.   [21] B adds and all the wild beasts and all the fourfooted things.

LVI. 2. Cf. xxii. 7, 8.
    LVII. 1. Cf. xxxvi. 1 ; Eth. En. xci. 1.   2. Riman, Ukhan, and

Khermion are not mentioned in i. 10.
On Gaidal, see i. 10 (note).
    LVIII. 1. When the Lord came

creeping things, and all the fowls that fly *in the air [1], and brought them all [1] before the face of our father Adam [2], and he gave names to all living things on the earth. 3. And the Lord made him lord over all, and put all things under his hands [3], and *subdued (them) to submission and to all obedience [4] *to man [5]. So the Lord created [6] man as master over all His possessions. 4. The Lord will not judge any soul of beast on account of man, *but he will judge the soul of man on account of the souls of beasts in the world to come [7]. 5. *For as there is a special place for mankind for all the souls of men according to their number, so there is also of beasts. And not one

---

[1] B om. [2] Sok. adds that he should give names to all fourfooted things. [3] Made subject to Adam all the newly created things, B.
[4] Secondly he placed all things under the rule of and made them obedient, B. Made them dumb and made them deaf to obey, A.
[5] As unto every man, Sok. [6] A adds every. [7] But the soul of man shall judge the animals in this world, A ; B gives the sense of the verse; but there shall not be a judgement of every living soul but only of that of man, and (?) in the great life to come.

---

upon the earth ... and visited. See xxxii. 1 (note). 5. Special place ... for all the souls of men. See xlix. 2 (note). So also of beasts. As the Jews believed at the beginning of the Christian era that all animals had spoken one language before the fall, and therefore in some degree possessed rationality (Jubilees iii. 28; Joseph. *Antt.* i. 1. 4), it was only natural that they should proceed to infer a future existence of the animal world. The O. T. indeed does not show a single trace of this belief, though it always displays a most tender solicitude for their well-being ; nor do we find it in any pre-Christian Jewish writing, with the exception of the present text. Even here the future life is of a limited nature. It is ethically motived. This further term of existence is not conceded for the brute's own sake, but wholly with a view to the punishment of man. The brute creation is to live just long enough to bring an indictment for ill-treatment against man at the final judgement. Though this idea of any future life in connexion with the brute creation may move the wonder of the modern mind, it is justified by perfectly analogous ideas in the ancient world. Not to speak of the doctrine of metempsychosis in Greece and the deification of animals in Egypt, such conceptions as those in the text would not unnaturally flow from the powers and qualities frequently assigned to animals by Greek thinkers. Thus, according to Plut. *Plac.* v. 20, 4, the souls of brutes were rational though

soul shall perish which God has made till the great judgement.   6. And every soul of beast shall bring a charge
against man if he feeds them badly[1].

---

[1] I have followed Sok. in verses 5, 6. B partly preserves the sense there
is one place and one fold for the souls of beasts. For every living
soul which God has made was not reserved for the great judgement.
And every soul of beasts, &c., as in text. A is transposed and corrupt;
There is a special place for mankind; as there is every soul of man
according to his number, so the beast also shall not perish. And every
soul of beast which God has made shall bring a charge against man at
(or until) the great judgement if, &c., as in text.

---

incapable of acting rationally on account of their bodies; according to
Xenocrates they possessed a consciousness of God, καθόλου γοῦν τὴν περὶ τοῦ
θείου ἔννοιαν Ξενοκράτης . . . οὐκ ἀπελ-
πίζει καὶ ἐν τοῖς ἀλόγοις ζῴοις (Clem.
Strom. v. 590). Chrysippus ascribed
reason to brutes (Chalkid in *Tim.*
p. 148 b); while Sextus Medicus
(ix. 127) maintained that the souls of
brutes and of men were alike. Hence
it was generally believed that the
souls of men could pass into brutes,
πρῶτον μὲν ἀθάνατον εἶναί φησι τὴν
ψυχήν, εἶτα μεταβάλλουσαν εἰς ἄλλα
γένη ζῴων (Porph. *V. P.* 19): while
Plato indeed went further and derived
the souls of all brutes ultimately from
those of men, through a process of
deterioration, ὡς γάρ ποτε ἐξ ἀνδρῶν
γυναῖκες καὶ τἆλλα θηρία γενήσοιντο,
ἠπίσταντο οἱ ξυνιστάντες ἡμᾶς (*Tim.*
76 D). With regard to individual
animals, some thinkers believed that
bees contained a divine element (Virg.
Georg. iv. 219-221), while Democri-
tus and Pliny placed religion among
the moral virtues of elephants (*H. N.*
viii. 1). But the closest parallels are
to be found in Zoroastrianism, to
which indeed we should probably
trace in some measure the ideas of
the text. Thus in the Zend-Avesta

Vendidad *Fargard* 13 (Darmesteter)
we find an entire chapter dealing with
the sacredness of the life of the domes-
ticated dog and the crime of attempt-
ing its life—its murderer was to lose
his soul to the ninth generation (1–4):
with the food that was to be given to
it and the penalties entailed by feed-
ing it badly (20–28), which were to
range from fifty to two hundred blows
with the horse-goad. Nay more, the
land, its pastures and crops were to
suffer for the unatoned death of the
dog, and these plagues were not to be
removed till the man who had slain
it was slain in turn or had offered
sacrifices three days and three nights
to the pious soul of the departed dog
(54, 55). Finally, the soul of the dog
went after death to the source of the
waters (51). In the *Midrash Koheleth*,
fol. 329, col. 1, we find the following
quaint and slightly analogous thought:
' Rabbi Chama, the son of Gorion,
said that wolves and unfruitful trees
must give account: just as man must
give account, so also must unfruitful
trees.' Eisenmenger, i. 468. It is
noteworthy that the ideas of the text
have passed over into the creed of the
Mohammedans. Thus, according to
Sale's note on the sixth chapter of
the Koran, irrational animals will be

[*Enoch teaches all his Sons why they must not touch the
Flesh of Cattle, because of what comes from it.*]

LIX. 1. He, who acts lawlessly with regard to the souls
of beasts, acts lawlessly with regard to his own soul.
2. For a man offers clean animals * and makes his sacrifice
that he may preserve his soul[1]. And if he offer as a sacrifice
from clean * beasts and[2] birds[3], he preserves his soul.
3. Everything that[4] is given you for food, bind by the
four feet: that is an atonement: he acts righteously (therein)
and preserves his soul.   4. But he who kills a beast
without a wound kills his own soul and sins against his

LIX. [1] And then he preserves his soul, B.   [2] B om.   [3] A adds it
is a salvation for man.   [4] A om. ; B OMITS VERSES 3, 4, 5.

---

restored to life at the resurrection that
they may be brought to judgement
and have vengeance taken on them
for the injuries they had inflicted on
each other in this life. Then after
they have duly retaliated their several
wrongs, God will turn them again to
dust (Sale's Koran, Prelim. Discourse,
Sect. iv), with the exception of Ezra's
ass and the dog of the seven sleepers
which will enjoy eternal life in Paradise (Koran iii; xviii). Are we to
interpret in this manner Orac. Sibyll.
viii. 415-418?—

κaὶ ὕστερον ἐς κρίσιν ἥξω
κρίνων εὐσεβέων καὶ δυσσεβέων βίον
ἀνδρῶν·
καὶ κριὸν κριῷ καὶ ποιμένι ποιμένα θήσω
καὶ μόσχον μόσχῳ πέλας ἀλλήλων ἐς
ἔλεγχον.

Even in Christian times animals were
credited with intelligence, conscience,
responsibility, as well as with the
passions, vices and virtues of mankind (see *Bestie delinquenti*, D'Addo-
sio, 1892, from which the following

facts are taken). They were accordingly solemnly tried, and advocates
were assigned at the public expense
to them to plead their cause. Thus
moles (824 A. D.), a sow (1324), a cock
(1474), snails (1487) were duly tried
and condemned. They were also
occasionally subjected to torture, and
their cries were regarded as a con-
fession of guilt (l. c. p. 46). Even as
late as 1531 a book was written by
Chassauée to discuss the lawfulness of
trying animals judicially, and the
legitimate methods of procedure
(l. c. p. 75).

LIX. 1. He who acts lawlessly,
&c.   At first sight this would seem to
refer to the sin of bestiality, and such
was the view of the scribe of A: see
title, but the context is against this,
as verses 2-4 clearly show. Hence
some illegitimate method of sacrificing
or slaughtering animals seems to be
referred to here. **2, 3.** These verses
point to a date prior to the destruction of the temple, 70 A.D. **4. Against**

own flesh.   5. And if any one does an injury to an animal secretly, it is an evil custom and he sins against his soul.

[*How we ought not to kill a Man, neither with Weapon nor with Tongue* [1].]

LX. 1. If he does an injury to the soul of man, he does an injury to his own soul; and there is no salvation for his flesh, * nor forgiveness [2] for ever [3].   2. He who kills the soul of a man, kills his own soul, and destroys his own body, and there is no salvation for him for ever.   3. He who prepares a net for another man * will fall into it himself and there is no salvation for him for ever [4].   4. He, who prepares a weapon against a man, shall not escape punishment in the great judgement for ever.   5. If a man acts crookedly or speaks evil against any soul, he shall have no righteousness for himself for ever.

[*Enoch admonishes his Sons to preserve themselves from Unrighteousness, and to stretch out their hands frequently to the Poor, and to give them something from their Labours.*]

LXI. 1. Now therefore, my children, preserve your hearts from every unrighteousness which the Lord hates.   As a man asks his soul from God, so let him do to every living soul [5].   2. * For in the world to come [2], * I know all things

---

LX. [1] A inserts this title after verse 1.   [2] B om.   [3] B adds but when a man is in Paradise he is liable to judgement no more.   [4] Shall not lose the punishment for it in the day of judgement for ever, Sok. B OMITS VERSES 2–5.

LXI. [5] B adds Even if it be not for eternal life.

---

strangling beasts. 5. Bestiality may be here referred to.

LX. 1. The sin referred to in 1 Thess. iv. 6. 3. Cf. Pss. ix. 15; xxxv. 8; lvii. 6. In this verse and the next two there is an utter want of proportion between the sin

and its punishment.   5. Cf. Ps. ci. 5.

LXI. 1. Unrighteousness which the Lord hates. Cf. Jud. v. 17; Ecclus. xv. 11, 13. 2. In the world to come ... many mansions. Cf. Eth. En. xxxix. 4, 7, 8; xli. 2; John

how that[1] there are many mansions prepared for men; *good for the good; evil for the evil; many and without number[2]. 3. Blessed are those who shall go to the mansions of the blessed[3]; for in the evil ones there is no rest nor any means of return from them. 4. Listen, my children, both small and great: When a man *conceives a good thought in his heart and brings[4] gifts before the Lord of his labours—if his hands have not wrought them[5] then the Lord turns away His face from the labour of his hands, and *he cannot gain advantage from[6] the work of his hand. 5. But if his hands have wrought, but his heart murmurs *and he does not make an offering of his heart, but murmurs[7] continually, he has no success.

[*How it is proper to bring one's Gifts with Faith, and how there is no Repentance after Death.*]

LXII. 1. Blessed is the man who in patience shall bring

---

[1] I know that, Sok.; B om.   [2] **Numberless** abodes for the good and the evil, B.   [3] B OMITS THE REST OF THE CHAPTER.   [4] **Sets** it in his heart to bring, Sok.   [5] The labour, Sok.   [6] It is impossible for him to find, Sok.   [7] The sickness of his heart will not cease and making a murmur, Sok.

---

xiv. 2. Good for the good, evil for the evil. This is adapted from Ecclus. xxxix. 25 ἀγαθὰ τοῖς ἀγαθοῖς ἔκτισται ἀπ' ἀρχῆς, οὕτως τοῖς ἁμαρτωλοῖς κακά. Cf. Or. Sibyll. Fragm. iii. 18–19 τοῖς ἀγαθοῖς ἀγαθὸν προφέρων πολὺ πλείονα μισθόν, τοῖς δὲ κακοῖς ἀδίκοις τε χόλον. 4. The text seems corrupt. The idea is: it is a good thing to offer gifts to God; but if a man sacrifice to God that which is another man's or is gotten wrongfully, God turns away His face from him. Cf. lxvi. 2. The author appears to have had before him Ecclus. xxxi. 21 θυσιάζων ἐξ ἀδίκου, προσφορὰ μεμωκημένη, 22 καὶ οὐκ εἰς εὐδοκίαν μωκήματα ἀνόμων. 23 οὐκ εὐδοκεῖ ὁ ὕψιστος ἐν προσφοραῖς ἀσεβῶν.

Further in ver. 24 ὁ προσάγων θυσίαν ἐκ χρημάτων πενήτων is condemned. Finally with he cannot gain advantage from, &c., compare ver. 28 τί ὠφέλησαν πλεῖον ἢ κόπου; If his hands have not wrought them. Cf. Or. Sibyll. viii. 403, 406:
τούτῳ μὲν καθαρὴν θὲς ἀναίμακτόν τε τράπεζαν
ἐκ μόχθων ἰδίων πορίσας ἁγναῖς παλάμῃσιν.

5. Men must offer willingly: only those are blessed. Cf. Exod. xxv. 2; xxxv. 5; Prov. xi. 25. But his heart murmurs. Cp. lxiii. 2; Deut. xv. 10 'thine heart shall not be grieved when thou givest unto him.' Ecclus. xxxii. 10, 11 ἐν ἀγαθῷ ὀφθαλμῷ δόξασον τὸν κύριον . . . καὶ ἐν εὐφροσύνῃ ἁγίασον δεκάτην.

his gifts[1] before the face of the Lord, for he shall avert
the recompense of his sin.   2. *If he speaks words out
of season[2] *there is no repentance for him: if he lets the
appointed time[3] pass and does not *perform the work, he
is not blessed; for[4] there is no repentance after death.
3. For every deed which a man does *unseasonably is[5] an
offence before men, and a sin before God.

[*How one must not despise the Humble, but give to them truly,
so that thou mayest not be accursed before God.*]

LXIII. 1. When a man clothes the naked and feeds the
hungry, he gets a recompense from God.   2. If his heart
murmurs, *he works for himself a double evil: he works
destruction to that which he gives and there shall be no
reward for it[6]:   3. *And the poor man, when his heart
is satisfied or his flesh is clothed[7] and he acts contemptuously,
he destroys the effect of *all his endurance of poverty[8] and
*shall not gain the blessing of a recompense[9].   4. For
the Lord hates every contemptuous *and proud-speaking[10]
man: *and likewise every lying word: and that which is
covered with unrighteousness. And it is cut with the
sharpness of a deadly sword, and thrown into the fire, and
burns for ever[11].

LXII. [1] A adds with faith.   [2] If he remembers the appointed time
to utter his prayer, B. If before the time he recalls his word, Sok.
[3] B omits, AND ALSO THE REST OF THE CHAPTER.   [4] Act righteously, A.
[5] Before the time and after the time is altogether, Sok.
LXIII. [6] He works for himself a double destruction and when he
gives anything to a man there shall be no reward for that which he has
given, A. B reads He renders his deeds of mercy profitless.   [7] Nay
more if food fill his heart to the full or his flesh is clothed, A. If he be-
comes overfed. B.   [8] His good works, B.   [9] Does not return with
gratitude the benefits he has received, A. Gains nothing, B.   [10] B om.
[11] And every lying word is sharpened with unrighteousness, and is cut
with the sharpness of a deadly sword, and that cutting has no healing
for ever, Sok. B om.

LXII. 1. Forgiveness is not the
message of this book. For most sins
there is no pardon. 2. Words out
of season. The text is hopeless here.

LXIII. 1. See ix (notes). 2.
See lxi. 5 (note). 4. The Lord
hates, &c. Pss. xviii. 27; ci. 5;
Prov. vi. 16, 17.

[*How the Lord calls Enoch: the People take Counsel to go to kiss him in the Place called Achuzan.*]

LXIV. 1. When Enoch said these words to his sons, *and the princes of the people [1], all the people *far and near [2] heard how the Lord called Enoch. And [3] they took counsel, *and they all said [4]: 'Let us go and kiss Enoch!' 2. And the men assembled to the number of 2000 [5], and came to the place Achuzan [6], where Enoch was, and his sons. 3. And [7] the elders of the people [8] *came together and made obeisance and [9] kissed Enoch, and said to him: '*Enoch, our father [9]; be thou blessed of the Lord, the eternal King!' 4. And now bless thy *sons, and all the [9] people, that we may be glorified *before thee to-day. 5. For thou art glorified [9] before the face of the Lord *for ever [1]; since God has chosen thee *above all men upon the earth, and has appointed thee [9] as *the scribe of His creation of visible and invisible things, and [9] an avenger [10] of the sins of men, *and a succour to thy family [9]!' And Enoch answered all his people saying [9]:

[*Of the Exhortation of Enoch to his Sons.*]

LXV. 1. 'Listen, my children: before that anything existed *and all creatures were made, the Lord made [11] all things both visible and invisible. 2. *When the times of these things

---

LXIV. [1] A om. [2] And all his neighbours, B. For how the Lord, B reads how the Lord God. [3] A B om. [4] Saying, B; A om. [5] 4000, B. [6] Asukhan, B. [7] A adds all the host of. [8] Sok. adds and all the host. [9] B om. [10] One who removes, A B. XLV. [11] The Lord made the world and then created, B. The Lord made, A.

LXIV. 5. **Scribe of His creation.** See xl. 13 (note); liii. 2. **Avenger, &c.** This may refer to Enoch's office at the final judgement when he recounts all the deeds of men. See quotation from Test. Abraham given in note on XL. 13. The reading, however, of A B one who removes may be right. Enoch may be conceived as a mediator. Cf. Philo's conception of the Logos i. 501.

LXV. 1. **Made.** This must mean

had come and were passed, understand how [1] after all these things He made man in His own image * after His [1] likeness, and placed in him eyes to see; and ears to hear; and a heart to understand, and reason [2] to take counsel.   3. And the Lord * contemplated the world for the sake of man [3], and made all the creation * for his sake [4], and divided * it into times. And from the times He made years, and from the years He made months, and from the months He made days, and of the days He made seven.   4. And in these He made the hours [5] * and divided them into small portions [1], that a man should understand * the seasons, and compute years and months, and hours; their alternations and beginnings and ends: and [6] that he should compute * his life from the beginning till death [7], * and should meditate upon his sin, and should write down his evil and good deeds. 5. For nothing done is concealed before the Lord. Let each man know his deeds, and not transgress the commandments and let him keep My writings securely from generation to generation [1].   6. When * all the creation of visible and invisible things [8] comes to an end which the Lord has made; then every man shall come to the great judgement of the Lord [9].   7. Then [10] the times shall perish, * and

---

[1] B om.   [2] **With his mind, A.**   [3] **Saw all the works of man,** A.   B om.   [4] A om.   B transposes it into next sentence.   [5] **Time** for the sake of man, and determined the times and the years, and the months and the hours, B.   [6] The changes of the times and the end and the beginning of the years, and the end and the days and hours, B.   [7] The death of his life, B.   [8] **The world, B.**   [9] A om. [10] **And then all, A.**

' devised,' if it is original. 2. **Made man in his own image . . . understand.** This agrees too closely to be accidental with Ecclus. xvii. 3 κατ᾿ εἰκόνα αὐτοῦ ἐποίησεν αὐτούς. 5. . . . ὀφθαλμούς, ὦτα καὶ καρδίαν ἔδωκε διανοεῖσθαι αὐτοῖς. 4. **Understand the seasons . . . beginnings and ends.** We have here a close resem-blance to Wisdom vii. 17–18 αὐτὸς γὰρ ἔδωκε . . . εἰδέναι . . . ἀρχὴν καὶ τέλος καὶ μεσότητα χρόνων, τροπῶν ἀλλαγὰς καὶ μεταβολὰς καιρῶν. 5. See xxxiii. 9 (note). 6. The judgement closes the existence of man on earth. At this judgement all men must appear, but there is nothing to suggest that there is a resurrection of the body. 7. See

there shall be no year, nor month, nor day, and there shall
be no hours nor shall they be reckoned[1].   8. There shall
be one eternity, and all the just *who shall escape the great
judgement of the Lord [2] shall be gathered together in eternal
life *and for ever and ever the just shall be gathered
together and they shall be eternal [3].   9. Moreover there
shall be no labour, nor sickness, nor sorrow, *nor anxiety,
nor need[4], nor night, nor darkness, but a great [5] light.
10. *And there shall be to them a great wall that cannot
be broken down[2]; and bright [6] *and incorruptible [2] paradise
*shall be their protection, and their eternal habitation[7].
*For all corruptible things shall vanish[2], *and there shall
be eternal life [8].

[*Enoch instructs his Sons, and all the Elders of the People : how
with Fear and Trembling they ought to walk before the
Lord, and serve Him alone, and not to worship Idols ; for
God made Heaven and Earth and every Creature and its
Form.*]

LXVI. 1. And now, my children, preserve your souls from
all unrighteousness, which the Lord hates[9]. Walk before
His face with fear *and trembling[10], and serve Him alone.

---

[1] And the years moreover shall perish and the months and days
and hours shall be dispersed and moreover shall not be counted, Sok.
For hours . . . counted A reads there shall be no hours nor shall there be
any addition to them or calculation. [2] B om. [3] And there shall be one
everlasting time for the just and they shall live for ever, A.   And
there shall be everlasting life for the just, being eternal, Sok. After
eternal B adds and incorruptible.   [4] A adds nor violence ; Sok. reads
nor necessary anxiety nor constraint.   [5] B adds unending and never
disturbed.   [6] Great, B Sok.   [7] B om. Sok. reads and there shall
be the roof of the eternal habitation, and transposes to end of Chapter.
[8] And incorruptible things shall come, Sok.   [10] Sok. om.
LXVI. [9] B OMITS THE REST OF THE CHAPTER.

---

xxxiii. 2. 8–9. A blessed immortality. 10. Wall. This may be the
wall that divides Paradise (see ix)
from the place of punishment (see x).
11. Cp. Ecclus. xiv. 19 τῶν ἔργον
σηπόμενον ἐκλείπει.

LXVI. 1. Unrighteousness
which the Lord hates. Cf. Deut.
xii. 31; Wisdom xiv. 9. Walk
before His face with fear and
trembling. Cf. Phil. ii. 12 'work
out your own salvation with fear and

* Worship the true God, and not dumb idols.   2. But
pay attention to His command [1], and bring every just offering before the face of the Lord. But the Lord hates that
which is unrighteous.   3. For the Lord sees every thing ;
whatever man meditates in his heart, * and what counsel
he plans [2], and every thought is continually before the Lord.
4. * If ye look at the heavens there is the Lord, as the Lord
made the heavens. If ye look at the earth then the Lord
is there since the Lord made firm the earth and established
every creature in it [3]. If ye scrutinize the depths of the sea,
and every thing under the earth there also is the Lord.
For the Lord created all things.   5. Do not bow down
to the work of men, * nor to the work of the Lord [4], leaving
* the Lord of all creation [5] ; for no deed is concealed before
the face of the Lord.   6. Walk, my children, in long
suffering, in humility [6], in spite of calumny, and insult ; in
faith, and truth : in the promises, and sickness, in abuse,
in wounds, in temptation, * in nakedness, in deprivation [7],
loving one another, till ye depart from this world of sickness.
Then ye shall be heirs of eternity.   7. Blessed are the
just, who shall escape the great judgement [8] ! And they
shall be seven times brighter than the sun, for in this age
altogether the seventh part is separated.   8. (Now concerning) the light, the darkness, the food, the sweetnesses,

---

[1] Sok. om.   [2] Then his reason counsels, Sok.   [3] So Sok. transposed
and defective in A. Who made firm the earth, and established every
creature in it. If ye look at the heavens there is the Lord   [4] A om.
[5] The works of the Lord, A.   [6] A adds honour.   [7] Deprivation and
nakedness, Sok.   [8] Sok. adds of the Lord.

---

trembling.' For fear and trembling
cf. also 2 Cor. vii. 15 ; Eph. vi. 5.
2. Bring every just offering. See
lxi. 4 (note). 3. Sees every thing
whatever man meditates, &c. Cf.
1 Chron. xxviii. 9 ; 2 Chron. vi. 30 ;
Ps. xciv. 11 ; Prov. xv. 11 ; Dan. ii.
30. 4. Founded partly on Ps. cxxxix.

8–12. The author has rightly omitted
all reference to Sheol as this is already
included in his conception of the
heavens. 5. No deed is concealed,
&c. Cf. Jer. xvi. 17 ; Ecclus. xvii. 15.
6. Cf. Rom. viii. 35 ; 2 Cor. xi. 27 ;
2 Pet. 1. 4. 7. Cf. lxv. 8. 8. Sweetnesses, &c. Eth. En. lxix. 8.

the bitternesses, the paradise, the tortures, *the fires, the frosts and other things[1]; *I have put[2] all this down in writing, that ye may read and understand.

[*The Lord sent a Darkness upon the Earth, and covered the People and Enoch; and he was taken up on high; and there was Light in the Heavens.*]

LXVII. 1. When Enoch had discoursed with the people, the Lord sent a darkness upon the earth, and there was a gloom, and it hid those men standing[3] with Enoch.   2. And *the angels hasted and took Enoch and carried him[4] to the highest heaven where the Lord[5] received him, and set him before *His face[6], and the darkness departed from the earth, and there was light.   3. And the people saw and did not understand, how Enoch was taken, and they glorified God. And they *who had seen such things[7] departed[8] to their houses[9].

LXVIII. 1. Enoch was born on the sixth day of the month Tsivan[10] ! he lived 365 years. He was taken up into heaven on the first day of the month Tsivan[11], and he was in heaven sixty days.   2. He wrote down the descriptions of all the creation which the Lord had made, and he wrote 366 books, and gave them to his sons.   3. And he was on earth

---

. [1] Sok. om.   [2] Put, A.

LXVII. [3] A adds and talking.   [4] They took him, A.   [5] A adds is and they.   [6] The face of the Lord, A.   [7] Sok. om. A reads Found the roll in which was the instruction concerning the invisible God and they.   [8] A adds all.   [9] B adds and concludes with to our God be glory for ever, Amen.

LXVIII. [10] Pamorus, Sok.   [11] Nisan, Sok.

LXVII. 2. Highest heaven. This is an exceptional privilege; for Paradise in the third heaven is the eternal abode of the righteous. See

LV. 2. In Asc. Is. ix. 7 the seventh heaven is represented as the future habitation of the righteous.

thirty days[1], and thus he was taken to heaven in the same[2] month Tsivan[3] on the *same day the[2] sixth day; the day on which he was born, and the same hour.   4. As each man has *but a dark existence[4] in this life, so also is his beginning *and birth[5], and departure from this life. In what hour he began; in that he was born, and in that he departs.   5. And Methusalem hasted, and all[5] his brethren[6], the sons of Enoch, and built an altar in the place called Achuzan, *whence and when Enoch[7] was taken up *to heaven[5].   6. And they took[8] cattle, and invited all the people and sacrificed victims[9] before the face of the Lord. 7. *All the people came and the elders of the people; all the host of them to the festivity, and brought their gifts to the sons of Enoch, and made a great festivity, rejoicing and being merry for three days; praising God who had given such a sign by means of Enoch, who had found favour with Him. And that they should hand it down to their son's sons, from generation to generation, for ever. Amen[5].

---

[1] Sok. adds having spoken with them.   [2] A om.   [3] Pamorus, Sok.
[4] An equal nature, Sok.   [5] Sok. om.   [6] Sok. adds and all.   [7] Where, Sok.
[8] Sok. adds animals and.   [9] Victim, Sok.

APPENDIX.

THE following fragment of the Melchizedekian literature was found by Professor Sokolov in the chief MS. on which he has based his text. In this MS. it is given as an organic factor of the Slavonic Enoch. This is done by omitting all the words in A lxviii. 7, after 'merry for three days,' and then as we see below immediately proceeding 'And on the third day,' &c. No hint of this large addition is found in A or B, but Sokolov writes that it appears in several MSS. to which he had access. The reader will observe that in many passages it implies the Slavonic Enoch. The text is obviously corrupt in many places.

We have in this fragment a new form of the Melchizedek myth. For the other forms it took see Bible Dictionaries *in loc.* This fragment seems to be the work of an early Christian heretic as we may infer from iii. 34 ; iv. 8.

I. 1. And on the third day at the time of the evening the elders of the people spake to Methusalam saying : 'Stand before the face of the Lord, and before the face of all the people, and before the face of the altar of the Lord, and thou shalt be glorified among the people.' 2. And Methusalam answered his people : 'Wait, O men, until the Lord God of my father Enoch—shall himself raise up to himself, a priest over his people.' 3. And the people waited yet a night to no purpose on the place Akhuzan. 4. And Methusalam was near the altar, and prayed to the Lord and said, 'Oh ! only Lord of all the world, who hast taken my father Enoch, do thou raise up a priest for thy people, and teach their hearts to fear thy glory, and to do all according to thy will. 5. And Methusalam slept, and the Lord appeared to him in a nightly vision, and said to him 'Listen, Methusalam, I am the Lord God of thy father Enoch, hear the voice of this people, and stand before My altar and I will glorify thee before the face of all the people, and thou shalt be glorified all the days of thy life.' 6. And Methusalam arose from his sleep, and blessed the Lord who had appeared to him.   7. And the elders of the people hastened to Methusalam and the Lord God inclined the heart of Methusalam to hear the voice of the people, and he said: 'The Lord God gives His blessing upon all these people before my eyes to-day. (May the Lord your God) do what is a good thing in His eyes to this people.'   8. And Sarsan and Kharmis, and Zazus, the elders of the people hastened and clothed Methusalam in beautiful garments and placed a bright crown on his head.   9. And the people hastened, and brought sheep and cattle and of birds all that was known (to be proper for) Methusalam to sacrifice before the face of the Lord, and in the name (before the face) of the people.   10. And Methusalam went out to the altar of the Lord, and his face shone like the sun, as it is rising in the day, and all the people were following after him.   11. And Methusalam stood before the altar of the Lord. and all the people stood round the altar.   12. And the elders of the people took sheep, and oxen, and bound their four feet, and laid them on the top of the altar, and said to Methusalam ;   13. 'Lift the knife and kill them according to the proper way before the face of the Lord.'   14. And Methusalam stretched out his hands to the heavens and called to the Lord, saying thus: 'Woe is me, O Lord! who am I to stand at the head of Thy altar and at the head of these people.   15. Now, Lord, look down on Thy servant and on all these people. Now let all the things sought for happen and give a blessing to Thy servant before the face of all the people, that they may understand that thou hast appointed a priest over Thy people.   16. And it came to pass that when Methusalam had prayed, the altar shook, and a knife rose from the altar, and leaped into the hand of Methusalam before the face of all the people. And the people trembled, and glorified the Lord.   17. And Methusalam was honoured before the face of the Lord, and before the face of all the people from that day.   18. And Methusalam took the knife, and killed every thing that was brought by the people. And they rejoiced, and were merry before the face of the Lord and before the face of Methusalam on that day.   19. And afterwards the people departed each to his own house.

II. 1. Methusalam began to stand at the altar before the face of the Lord and all the people from that day for ten years, trusting in an eternal inheritance, and having taught well the whole land and all his people; and no man was found to turn from the Lord in vanity during all the days in which Methusalam lived.   2. And the Lord blessed Methusalam and was pleased with his sacrifices, and his gifts and all his services which he served before the face of the Lord. 3. And when the time of the days of the departure of Methusalam took place, and the Lord appeared to him in a nightly vision, and said to him: 'Listen, Methusalam! I am the Lord God of thy father Enoch, I order thee to see, how the days of thy life are finished, and the day of thy rest has drawn near. 4. Call Nir, the son of thy son Lamech, the second, born after Noah, and clothe him in the robes of thy consecration, and place him by my altar, and tell him all that shall be in his days, because the time of the destruction of the whole earth draws near, and of every man and every living thing upon the earth. 5. For in his days there shall be a very great confusion upon the earth, because a man has been envious of his neighbour, and people have become inflamed against people and nation stirs up war against nation, and all the earth is filled with foulness and blood, and every kind of evil. 6. And moreover in addition they deserted their Maker, and have bowed down to vain gods, and to the firmament of heaven, and the course of the earth and the waves of the sea. And the adversary is multiplied and rejoices in his deeds to My great vexation. 7. And all the earth changes its form, and every tree and every fruit changes its seeds, expecting the time of destruction. And all peoples are changing upon the earth to My grief. 8. Then I shall command the abysses to pour themselves upon the earth, and the great treasuries of the waters of heaven shall come upon the earth in their nature and according to their first nature. 9. And all the stability of the earth shall perish and all the earth shall tremble and shall be deprived of its strength from that day. 10. Then I will preserve the son of thy son Lamech, his first son Noe and from his seed I will raise up another world, and his seed shall exist for ever till the second destruction when also men shall sin before my face. 11. Methusalam leaped up from his sleep and his dream troubled him greatly. And he called all the elders of the people and told them all that the Lord had said to him, and all the vision that had appeared to him from the Lord. 12. And the people were grieved at his vision, and answered him: 'Let the Lord God do according to his will! And now, Methusalam, accomplish thou all things which the Lord enjoined thee.' 13. And Methusalam called Nir, the son of Lamech, the younger brother of Noe, and clothed him in the robes of the priesthood before the face of all the people, and placed him at the head of the altar, and taught him all that he was to do among the people. 14. And

Methusalam called to the people: 'Lo! Nir will be before your face from to-day as a prince and a leader.' 15. And the people said to Methusalam, 'Let it be unto us according to thy word, and let the voice of the Lord be as He spoke to thee.' 16. And when Methusalam had spoken to the people before the altar, his spirit was confused, and he bent his knees, and stretched out his hands to the heavens, and prayed to God. And as he prayed his spirit went forth to the Lord. 17. And Nir and all the people made haste and made a grave for Methusalam in the place Aruzan. 18. And Nir came in glorious attire in all his priestly robes, with lights, with much pomp, and the people lifted up the body of Methusalam, and having glorified it, laid it in the grave, which they had made for him, and buried him, and said: 'Blessed was Methusalam before the face of the Lord, and before the face of all people.' 19. When they were about to depart to their own households, Nir said to the people: 'Go quickly now, and bring sheep and heifers, and turtle-doves, and pigeons, and let us offer them before the face of the Lord, and then go to your houses.' 20. And the people listened to Nir the priest, and hastened and brought the victims, and bound them to the head of the altar. 21. And Nir took the sacrificial knife, and slew all the [victims] that were brought, and offered them before the face of the Lord. 22. And all the people rejoiced before the face of the Lord, and glorified on that day the Lord of Nir, the ruler of heaven and earth. From that day there was peace and order over the whole earth in the days of Nir, during 202 years. 23. And then the people turned from God and began to be jealous one of another, and people rebelled against people, and tongue arose against tongue, in reviling. 24. And if lips were the same, hearts chose different things. 25. And then the devil began to reign for the third time, the first time before paradise, the second time in paradise, the third time outside of paradise, he continued (doing so) till the deluge. 26. And there arose a great dispute and confusion. And Nir the priest heard it, and was greatly grieved, and said in his heart, 'In truth I have understood that the time has drawn near, and the end which the Lord spake to Methusalam, the father of my father Lamech.

III. 1. And the wife of Nir, named Sopanima, being barren, brought forth no child to Nir. 2. And Sopanima was in the time of her old age, and on the day of her death she conceived in her womb, and Nir the priest did not sleep with her, nor knew her from the day that the Lord appointed him to serve before the face of the people. 3. When Sopanima knew of her conception she was ashamed, and felt humbled, and concealed herself all the days, till she brought forth, and no one of the people knew. 4. And when 282 days were accomplished and the day of birth began to draw near, Nir remembered about his wife, and called her to himself in his house, that he might talk to her. 5. And Sopanima came to Nir, her husband, being with child, and the appointed day of the birth was drawing near. 6. And Nir saw her and was very much ashamed, and said to her : ' What hast thou done, wife, and hast shamed me before the face of these people. And now depart from me, and go where thou didst commence the shame of thy womb, so that I defile not my hand upon thee, and sin before the face of the Lord ! ' 7. And Sopanima spake unto Nir, her husband, saying : ' My lord, lo ! the time of my old age, and the day of my death has come (and there was no youth in me) and I do not know when the period of my years is past, and the unfruitfulness of my womb begin.' 8. And Nir did not believe his wife, and said to her a second time: ' Depart from me lest I do thee an injury, and sin before the face of the Lord ! ' 9. And it came to pass, when Nir had spoken to his wife, Sopanima fell at the feet of Nir, and died. 10. And Nir was very much grieved, and said in his heart : ' Was this from my voice, since a man by his voice and thought sins before the face of the Lord. 11. Now the Lord is merciful to me ; I know in truth in my heart, that my hand was not upon her. And so I say : " Glory to thee, oh ! Lord, since no one on earth knows this deed, which the Lord has wrought ! " ' 12. And Nir hastened and shut the doors of the house, and went to Noe, his brother, and told him all, that had happened concerning his wife. 13. And Noe hastened, and came with Nir, his brother, into the house of Nir, on account of the death of Sopanima, and they talked to themselves (and saw) how her womb was at the time of the birth. 14. And Noe said to Nir : ' Let it not be a subject of sorrow to thee, Nir, my brother, that the Lord has to-day concealed our shame because no one of the people knows this. 15. Now let us go quickly, and bring her secretly, and may the Lord hide the ignominy of our shame. 16. And they laid Sopanima on the bed, and they wrapped her with black robes, and shut her in the house ready for burial, and dug a grave in secret. 17. And then came an infant from the dead Sopanima, and sat on the bed at her right hand. And Noe, and Nir entered, and saw the infant sitting by the dead Sopanima and wiping its clothes.   18. And Noe, and Nir were tempted with a great fear, for the child was complete in its body, like one of three years old; and spake with its lips, and blessed the Lord. 19. And Noe, and Nir gazed upon it; and lo! the seal of the priesthood was on its breast, and it was glorious in countenance. 20. And Noe, and Nir said ' See the Lord renews the consecration according to our blood, as he desires (this is from the Lord, my brother, and the Lord renews the blood of consecration in us).' 21. And Noe and Nir hastened, and washed the child, and clothed it in priestly raiment, and gave it the blessed bread. And it ate.   And they called its name Melchizedek.   22. And Noe and Nir took the body of Sopanima, and stripped from her the black robes, and clothed her in very bright robes, and built a church for her (another house—a beautified grave).   .23. And Noe, and Nir, and Melchizedek came and buried her publicly.   And Noe said to his brother Nir : ' Watch this child in secret till the time, because deceitful people shall arise over all the earth and shall begin to reject God, and having perceived nothing shall put him to death.   And then Noe went out to his own place.   24. And great lawlessness began to multiply over the whole earth, in the days of Nir.   25. And Nir began to be very anxious, especially about the child, saying : ' Woe is me, eternal Lord.   In my days have begun to multiply all kinds of lawlessness upon the earth, and I understand, how that the end is near unto us more (than ever), and upon all the earth for the lawlessness of the people.   26. And now, Lord, what is the vision, and what is the solution of it, and what shall I do for (the child) ?—Will it also go with us to destruction ? ' 27. And the Lord heard Nir, and appeared to him in a nightly vision, and said to him : ' Nir, I do not endure the great lawlessness that has been on the earth in many things, and lo ! I wish now to send a great destruction upon the earth, and every earthly creature shall perish.   28. But do not trouble thyself about the child, Nir, for in a short time I will send my chief captain Michael, and he shall take the child and place him in the paradise of Eden, in the garden where Adam was formerly during a period of seven years, having the heaven always open until the time of his sin. 29. And this child shall not perish with those who perish in this generation, as I have shown, but shall be a holy priest in all things, Melchizedek, and I will appoint him that he may be the chief of the priests who were before (*alia lectio*—that he may be a priest of priests for ever, and I will consecrate him, and will appoint him over the people being made greatly holy).   30. And

Nir rose from his sleep, and blessed the Lord, who had appeared unto him, saying : 'Blessed is the Lord God of my fathers, who has spoken unto me, (*some MSS. add*—who will not allow the depreciation of my priesthood in the priesthood of my fathers, as thy word), who made a great priest in my days in the womb of my wife Sopanima. (*Some MSS. add*—31. Because I had no family and this child shall be to me in the place of my family, and shall be as a son to me, and thou shalt honour him with Thy servants the priests, with Seth, and Enoch, and Tharasidam, Maleleil, and Enos, and thy servant, and thus Melchizedek shall be a priest in another generation. 32. For I know that this generation shall end in confusion, and all shall perish. And Noe, my brother, shall be preserved in that day. 33. And from my race shall rise up many people, and Melchizedek shall be the chief of the priests among the people, ruling alone, serving thee O Lord!) 34. Because I had not another child in this family, who might be a great priest, but this son of mine, and thy servant; and do thou great Lord, on this account honour him with thy servants, and great priests—with Seth, and Enos, and Rusii, and Almilam, and Prasidam, and Maleleil, and Seroch, and Arusan, and Aleem, and Enoch, and Methusalam, and me, thy servant Nir, and Melchizedek shall be the head over twelve priests who lived before, and at last shall be the head over all, (being) the great high priest, the Word of God, and the power to work great and glorious marvels above all that have been. 35. He, Melchizedek, shall be a priest and king in the place Akhuzan, that is to say, in the middle of the earth where Adam was created : there shall at last be his grave. 36. And concerning that chief priest it has been written that he also shall be buried there, where there is the middle of the earth, as Adam buried his son Abel there whom his brother Cain killed, wherefore he lay three years unburied, till he saw a bird called a jackdaw, burying its fledgling. 37. I know that a great confusion has come and this generation shall end in confusion, and all shall perish except that Noe my brother shall be preserved, and afterwards there shall be a planting from his family, and there shall be other people, and another Melchizedek shall be the head of the priests among the people, ruling, and serving the Lord.'

IV. 1. And when the child had been forty days under the roof of Nir, the Lord said to Michael :- 'Go down upon the earth to Nir, the priest, and take My child Melchizedek, who is with him, and place him in the paradise of Eden for preservation, because the time draws nigh, and I will discharge all the water upon the earth, and all that is upon the earth shall perish.   2. (And I will establish another race, and Melchizedek shall be the chief of the priests, in that family, just as Seth is to me in this family[1].') 3. And Michael hastened, and came by night, and Nir was sleeping in his bed.   And Michael appeared to him, and said to him: 'The Lord says unto thee, Nir : "Send the child to me; I entrusted him to thee."'   4. And Nir did not know that the chief captain Michael was speaking to him, and his heart was confused, and he said: 'If the people know about the child, and take him, they will slay him.   For the heart of this people is crafty before the face of the Lord.   And Nir said to him who spoke to him 'The child is not with me, and I do not know who thou art, who art speaking to me.'   5. And he who was speaking to me answered : 'Be not afraid, Nir, I am the chief captain of the Lord.   The Lord hath sent me, and lo! I will take thy child to-day, and will go with him, and will place him in the paradise of Eden, and there shall he be for ever. 6. And when the twelfth generation shall be, and a thousand and seventy years shall be, in that generation a just man shall be born, and the Lord shall tell him to come out upon that mountain where the ark of thy brother Noe shall stand, and he shall find there another Melchizedek who has lived there seven years, concealing himself from the people who worship idols, so that they should not slay him, and he shall lead him forth and he shall be priest, and the first king in the town of Salem after the fashion of this Melchizedek, the commencement of the priests.   And 3432 years shall be fulfilled till that time from the beginning and creation of Adam.   7. And from that Melchizedek there shall be twelve priests in number till the great Igumen, that is to say leader, who shall bring forth all things visible and invisible. 8. And Nir understood his first dream, and believed it, and having answered Michael, he said : 'Blessed is the Lord, who has glorified thee to-day to me, and now bless thy servant Nir, as we are drawing near our departure from this world, and take the child, and do unto him as the Lord hath spoken unto thee.   9. And Michael took the child on that night on which he came, and took him on his wings, and placed him in the paradise of Eden. 10. And Nir having risen on the following day, went to his house, and did not find the child, and there was instead of joy very great sorrow, because he had no other son except this (*alia lectio*—because he

---

[1] Clearly a variant of iii. 37.

looked upon this child in the place of a son). 11. So died Nir,
and after him there was no priest among the people. And from
that time a great confusion arose on the earth.

V. 1. And God called Noe on the mountain of Ararat, between
Assyria, and Armenia, in the land of Arabia, by the sea, and said
to him: 'Make there an ark of 300 ells in length, and in breadth
50 ells, and in height 30, and two stories in the midst, and the
doors about an ell. 2. And of those 300 ells, and of ours
15,000, and so of those 50, and of ours 2000 and 500, and so of
those 30, and of ours 900, and of those one ell, and of ours 50.'
3. According to this number the Jews keep this measure of the
ark of Noe, as the Lord said to him, and (so) they make each
measure, and each rule even up to the present time. 4. The Lord
God opened the doors of the heavens, and rain came on the earth
150 days, and all flesh died. 5. Noe was in the 500th year
and begat three sons: Shem, Ham, and Japhet. 6. 100 years
after the birth of his three sons, he went into the ark in the month
according to the Hebrew Itsars, according to the Egyptian Famenoth
in eighteen days. 7. And the ark floated forty days. And altogether they were in the ark 120 days. 8. And he went into
the ark, being 600 years (old), and in the sixth hundred and first
year of his life he went out of the ark in the month Farmut according to the Egyptians, and according to the Hebrews Nisan about
twenty-eight days. 9. Then he lived 250 years, and died; he lived
altogether 950 years according [to the will of] the Lord our God, to
him be glory from the beginning, and now, and to the end of the
world. Amen. 10. Enoch was altogether 365 years old.

11. In another way it is written here concerning Noah's ark.
Of their 300 ells, and of ours 15,000, of theirs 100, and of ours
5000 : of theirs 20, and of ours 1000 ; of theirs 10, and of ours 500 :
of theirs 5, and of ours 250 : of theirs 1, and of ours 50 ! This is
the truth spoken.

ADDITIONAL NOTE ON THE PHOENIXES..

WHEN I wrote the note on the Phoenixes in XII. 1 I was not aware that mention of a class of these birds was to be found elsewhere. I have, however, since found in Dr. Kohler's article on 'The pre-Talmudic Haggada' (*Jewish Quarterly*, 1893, pp. 399–419) a quotation from an old Essene Mishna— *Massecheth Derech Eretz*—in which it is said that 'the generation of the bird מלהם' went alive into Paradise. This bird Dr. Kohler identifies with the Phoenix. The question is discussed in the *Alphabetum Siracidis* edited by Steinschneider, 1858, p. 28b.

INDEX I.

PASSAGES FROM THE SCRIPTURES AND ANCIENT WRITERS
CONNECTED OR CLOSELY PARALLEL WITH THE TEXT.

— ❖ —

INDEX II.

NAMES AND SUBJECTS.

————◆◆————

(When thick type is used in this Index, it is to indicate that the subject in
question is specially dealt with under the reference so given.)

THE END.